healing from an emotionally absent mother

A WORKBOOK

Also by Jasmin Lee Cori, MS

The Emotionally Absent Mother: How to Recognize and Heal the Invisible Effects of Childhood Emotional Neglect

Healing from Trauma: A Survivor's Guide to Understanding Your Symptoms and Reclaiming Your Life

For a complete list, see jasmincori.com.

healing from an emotionally absent mother

Learn to Build Trust, Take in Nourishment, and Move Past the Wounds Left by Neglect

A WORKBOOK

JASMIN LEE CORI, MS

sheldon PRESS

First published in the United States by The Experiment, LLC in 2025.

First published in Great Britain by Sheldon Press in 2025
An imprint of John Murray Press

1

Copyright © Jasmin Lee Cori 2025

The right of Jasmin Lee Cori to be identified as the Author of the Work has been asserted by her in accordance with the Copyright, Designs and Patents Act 1988.

Cover and text design by Beth Bugler
Author photograph by Michael Teak

All rights reserved. No part of this publication may be reproduced, stored in a retrieval system, or transmitted, in any form or by any means without the prior written permission of the publisher, nor be otherwise circulated in any form of binding or cover other than that in which it is published and without a similar condition being imposed on the subsequent purchaser.

This book is for information or educational purposes only and is not intended to act as a substitute for medical advice or treatment. Any person with a condition requiring medical attention should consult a qualified medical practitioner or suitable therapist.

A CIP catalogue record for this title is available from the British Library

Trade Paperback ISBN 978 1 3998 2 221 3
ebook ISBN 978 1 3998 2 222 0

Typeset in Kepler Std

Printed and bound in Great Britain by Clays Ltd, Elcograf S.p.A.

John Murray Press policy is to use papers that are natural, renewable and recyclable products and made from wood grown in sustainable forests. The logging and manufacturing processes are expected to conform to the environmental regulations of the country of origin.

John Murray Press
Carmelite House
50 Victoria Embankment
London EC4Y 0DZ

www.sheldonpress.co.uk

John Murray Press, part of Hodder & Stoughton Limited
An Hachette UK company

The authorised representative in the EEA is Hachette Ireland, 8 Castlecourt Centre, Dublin 15, D15 XTP3, Ireland (email: info@hbgi.ie)

Contents

	Introduction	1
1	The Healing Journey	7
2	Tools for Doing the Work	13
3	Our Need for Mothering	23
4	The Mother of Your Childhood	35
5	Emotionally Absent and Emotionally Abusive Mothers	51
6	The Impacts of Being Under-Mothered	71
7	Trauma and Triggers	93
8	Claiming What Was Lost to You	107
9	The Deeper Emotional Work	119
10	Exploring Your Current Relationship with Mother	131
11	Parenting Your Young Parts	159
12	Self-Care as Mothering	169
13	Taking In Nourishment	183
14	Bringing the Healing Forward	199
15	Reflecting on Your Journey	209
	Acknowledgments	216
	About the Author	217

I dedicate this book to those of you willing to do the hard work to free yourself of the shackles of childhood emotional neglect and rise to feel the wind beneath your wings and be all that you are.

Introduction

Many of us leave childhood with psychological wounds we may not understand or even become aware of for a number of years. In this book we'll be focusing on childhood emotional neglect. Rather than the physical neglect of inadequate shelter, food, and supervision, emotional neglect involves inadequate levels of care and attunement to your emotional needs—every bit as damaging.

I introduced this topic in my earlier book, *The Emotionally Absent Mother*, which zeroed in on mothers who are not emotionally present to their children and thus cannot provide the psychological foundation a child needs. In this book, I extend that work by providing new material and by adopting a workbook format designed for those who want a more structured process for their healing work. You do not need to have read the earlier book to use this workbook, but it is a good complement, with additional context and real-life stories. It also has its own exercises, different from those here. Much of the material in this workbook is applicable to healing from any kind of childhood trauma and to emotional healing in general.

How Do You Know If You Were Emotionally Neglected?

There are two ways. One is to compare how you were mothered with descriptions of emotionally absent mothers. The other is to look for the feelings and impacts left by this kind of neglect. Here is an overview of things you might find.

Your mother was physically present (at least part of the time), but not really meeting you emotionally or doing all the things you may have noticed other mothers doing—like being really involved, there when you needed her, providing a sense of security, actively helping you with the challenges that came your way. If there were not enough of these mothering activities, we call that being *under-mothered*.

If you can't point to an abundance of good mothering activities or the kind of bond you think a mother and child should have, you may question, "How come I don't have warm feelings when I think of my mother? We were not close in the ways I would have wanted. I was not even sure that she loved me."

Other common impacts include difficulty knowing your feelings (because they were ignored or shamed), trouble with emotional regulation (tipping into extremes), depression, anxiety, and upset that push you to self-soothe with things like substance abuse.

Challenges in establishing close relationships and maintaining them over time, difficulty trusting, finding it hard to reveal yourself, and not feeling safe are all clues that the initial imprint was not a good one. Many who suffered this kind of neglect end up feeling emotionally starved for love.

Emotional neglect also shows up in your expectations in relationships. The two most common patterns are expecting little to nothing from others, or feeling others will only attend to you if they want something or if you force them to. It's just not familiar to you to receive positive attention and support—although you would very much like it.

If you didn't have a mother serving as a positive mirror, you are not likely to have a robust sense of self. Your self-esteem has holes in it, as does your confidence. You may feel tentative, not ready to take risks or tackle big projects.

In short, rather than feeling like you had a warm, safe home where you were fully nourished, you feel more like an orphan, or the child in the fairy tale "The Little Match Girl," freezing in the cold, her lit match the only warmth available.

You'll learn more about the deficits left by under-mothering in this workbook and, more important, how to heal the wounds left by an inattentive mother.

What Will You Find Here?

We'll start by describing what to expect from the healing journey and giving you the tools you need to do this work and stay safe.

The next chapters lay out why mothering is so important and help you uncover your own childhood experiences before looking at emotional absence and emotional abuse and deciphering how much of either or both was present in your childhood. We then begin a process of connecting the dots—what was missing in your childhood and what you struggle with today. Emotional neglect and abuse can both cause trauma, so we also look at complex trauma and how to identify it.

Looking at the past and uncovering feelings are only the first part of healing, so next we move on to making up for what you missed—teaching you how to become a better parent to your inner child, how to mother yourself now, and how to take in more emotional nourishment so that you can pay the healing forward.

With all of this under your belt, we return, at the end, to Mother—this time the mother of the present. Exercises help you assess your current relationship with Mother (if you have one) and what you would like to get from it from as realistic a perspective as possible. Finally, we'll reflect on how this work has changed you.

Using This Workbook

I invite you to do your work right here in the workbook, so you will want to secure your book (protect its privacy) so that you can be as open and honest as possible. It's also good to have a private space in which to work. I recommend a cozy, protected environment as free of interruptions as possible so that your emotions are free to come up and be expressed. The exercises can go quite deep, so you will also want to give yourself sufficient time to work with them.

If you're working along and come across an exercise or topic that feels a little too scary, you can save it for a time you feel more resourced (more centered and steady). You may have learned as a child to push through situations that you didn't really have the support for, and while that can come in handy in some situations, as a pattern, it is the opposite of the more attuned self-support that will serve you here. Better to pace your work and not push too hard. It is good to gradually expand your comfort zone, but if you go too far outside it, you can become destabilized. It's important to stop and support yourself before you get to that point. This requires that you maintain self-awareness and work within what is called your "window of tolerance," maintaining your sense of safety.

This workbook provides general scaffolding for a very individual process of growth. As you'll hear again and again, this is a healing journey. It is helping you shore up your foundation, and that cannot happen in a matter of days or weeks but rather months and years. A few chapters may go more quickly, but it will take you weeks to work with many of the chapters in a way that allows you to get the most out of them. You may even find yourself taking a break in the middle of them. That may be your natural intelligence telling you it's too soon to continue. This pacing is something you learn to trust.

Working in Groups

Some people like workbooks because they give you a chance to have complete privacy and do the work on your own. That is valid. You do not need to be in a group to use this book! Yet there are advantages to working with others, so this book is designed to make that an option as well.

Since the wounding of emotional neglect and abuse arises within relationships, healing relationships are an important part of the antidote. Doing the work with others who share this journey with you can help you feel supported and less alone. You learn from seeing how others face difficult things. With a group, you have a chance to give and receive (both good to practice), and you can be seen in life-affirming ways that change the way you see yourself.

To that end, I've designed the workbook so that it can be adopted by groups. These may be therapy groups, support groups, classes, or something you put together with a few friends. Many of the exercises can be modified for use with a single partner, and although there are advantages to working with others who are also walking this path, you can choose whoever feels safe to you.

This icon identifies exercises with specific instructions for group work. They maximize the value of having others as part of the process. You might skim them even if you are working on your own, as they may spur a new awareness or nudge you to find others to share an exercise with.

Do You Need to Work in Sequence?

It's hard to be linear with a process that involves many elements that ideally are all at work as you go along. These elements include having a baseline of knowledge about childhood emotional neglect, strategies for working with challenging emotions and memories, and skills for good self-care. Yet a book, by its nature, is linear, so we have to take these elements one by one.

The chapter sequence leads you through a progression of topics, and the early material lays the foundation for later work. Yet keeping in mind the need for all of these skills at different moments, feel free to move around when you recognize a need. If you see a topic up ahead that feels timely, give yourself permission to go there, but then double back. I suggest you not skip large sections. There may be some exercises you choose not to do, but I recommend you read the accompanying text for the information. You may find yourself coming back to the exercise at a later time.

Like every task in life, this is a chance to be a good mother to yourself, attuning to your needs, honouring your limitations, and taking the hand offered to you when it feels right. I hope that in this sacred healing process you strengthen and broaden the good mothering qualities in your life.

Welcome!

1

The Healing Journey

The Promise of Healing

Healing early childhood wounds is one of the longer journeys you can take in life. It's long because this wounding occurs before you have built a healthy foundation for yourself, so they are at your very core. When these childhood wounds are the result of what Mother didn't provide that you needed, or of harmful elements in your relationship with her, we call them "mother wounds."

You might think healing should happen a lot quicker—and some people will try to convince you that it can. But you can't just yank on a seedling and make it grow, and you can't force the growth involved in healing. It doesn't help to have expectations that frustrate you and make you feel bad. Let's be honest: Healing takes time and involves hard work.

At different stages in your healing journey, you might find yourself thinking the following.

- How the f*** did I get here?
- I don't know if I can make it. I don't know if I am strong enough.
- I'm afraid of my anger.
- How can I survive this depth of hurt?
- I'm tired of working through this.
- I'm starting to feel better. Can't I be done now?

There is a path through this, but it's not a path anyone can lay out in a linear way. It's much more individual and organic than that. No one can tell you how long it will take, and no professional can credibly say, "I can get you there in ten sessions." No book can cure you. What this workbook can do is support you in your work.

Healing from childhood emotional neglect is like putting together a 1,500-piece puzzle. There's no one right way to put it together. You work where you can or where you most need to. Often, life puts in front of you the next piece for you to deal with.

Because there is not a specific map to follow or a picture of the destination, let me give you a few benchmarks for what might *feel* different as you heal your mother wounds.

The biggest marker of healing is that you won't feel like you did as a child. The world outside won't feel the way it did for you then, and you won't feel the way you did when you were going through all that. You will be different. You will be a bigger you.

Won't that be nice! That's what growing up is supposed to be. Being an adult involves more than making your own decisions and being responsible for yourself. Growing up is *growing*. Upward. Outward. Bigger. Happier. Becoming your own person. That's true for all of us, but it's especially true when you haven't had a good foundation laid down by Mother.

This growing requires you to set down the load you were given to carry (we are all given something to carry), unpack it, and take a good look at what's in there. As you are looking—if you do it carefully and with as much courage and honesty as you can—it begins to sort itself out. You find that you no longer need to carry the grief (which, for much of your life, you didn't even know you were carrying). The heartache lightens. You let go of impossible hopes—for instance, that Mother will become something she is not.

As you do your work, you'll begin to fill up with the things you needed earlier but didn't get: people liking you, seeing you, enjoying you, holding you when you are sad. You'll feel encouraged—by those you surround yourself with, but also by the results of your own efforts. You'll learn to take really good care of yourself—and even enjoy doing so. You'll become stronger and more empowered. You'll no longer be the scrunched and scraped-up you that you've felt like all these years. Rather than being that small, lonely child, you'll actualize the potential you brought into this life. You'll become who you were meant to be.

This is the promise of healing.

My Story of Healing

Who am I to write about healing? I am someone who has had firsthand experience healing the wounds I describe here. I also worked for many years as a psychotherapist helping others to heal their wounds. Healing is what my life has been about.

It used to rankle me when authors of books about trauma would talk about the goal being to return to your pre-trauma functioning. What if there was no *before* trauma for you? What if you faced traumatizing events from the very get-go? That may be how it was for you. It is how it was for me.

The two major loads I was given to carry (and transform) were interwoven—they were married! They are represented by my father and mother: my father due to pervasive sexual abuse (described briefly in my book *Healing from Trauma*) and my mother due to emotional absence. It took decades for me to become conscious of these wounds and then much hard work and many years to heal.

With my mother wound, I'm in a good place now. I credit that to several factors. First, I continue to take in from other sources what I missed from my mother. Having carried a strong sense of aloneness much of my life, being seen and heard for who I am has been very healing to me. I was also graced with excellent therapists. All of this helped me through the painful work of facing what felt missing from Mum.

Another factor is that I do not carry the wound forward by holding myself to blame. I understand much more about why my mother was the way she was, and I don't think it was because of something I didn't do or couldn't be.

My relationship with my mother evolved in the last years of her life, when I became responsible for some of her care. This role reversal brought moments of tenderness on both sides, and the last words we said to each other were, "I love you" (words I don't remember hearing as a child). That was a moment that reflected our healing, and so I treasure it.

Primary Elements in the Healing Journey

The three main pillars of healing mother wounds, as I see them, are as follows.

Facing your truth. There is no healing journey without this. This is the beginning of your journey and it continues all the way through. It starts with facing how you experienced your mother, which may be very different from your family's story about her. Maybe you were always aware of these things, but maybe not. You must get below the defences that you used to protect yourself and feel the full impact of how your mother's neglect or abuse hurt you. This involves feeling the emotions that come with this recognition—emotions you have done your best to minimize or deny before now.

Understanding Mother. What was going on to make her act the way she did? If you don't understand what is behind Mother's behaviour, you'll tend to make up stories about it—and blame yourself! Children have very little life experience or ability to see the endless number of things that drive others' behaviour. They live in a tiny world with themselves in the middle, so they don't know that someone's behaviour often has nothing to do with them. A young child often believes, "If Mummy is mad, it must be because I did something bad" or "If Mummy doesn't love me, it's because something is wrong with me."

Making up for what you missed. It does no good to analyze and understand if you don't also bring in "good medicine." You can make up for these deficits by mothering yourself and taking in as much nourishment as you can.

What Does It Mean to Be Healed?

Being healed doesn't mean you never hurt again. You are healed to the extent that when hurt comes up, it is less and less devastating. The hurt comes up less frequently and is no longer a dominant presence. The narrative of your life changes as you leave the hurt behind.

Healing occurs in layers. A particular piece of content may appear multiple times, but generally (if we are indeed healing), we move to deeper and deeper layers of it. So, for example, you may recognize that you don't use your voice to stand up for yourself. Usually, your first attempts will be a bit clumsy, but you will get more skilled with practice. As you progress, the challenges will often become more advanced, and the ways you can stand up for yourself become more nuanced.

Therapists who do any kind of depth work understand healing as a spiral, going round and round through similar territory, but at deeper levels. You may think, "But I've already been there!" and feel discouraged. The task is then to discern whether you are truly spinning your wheels or if a different aspect of the issue is showing up this time. Although we can take this returning to familiar content as a failure, it's not. Big challenges and traumas generally travel with us, changing over time. When you want to blame yourself for returning to the same old issue, just imagine a grizzled old man smoking a cigar who looks at you and asks, "So how many issues did you want?"

You'll know you have progressed in your healing journey when you are able to become aware of an emotional trigger (anything that sets off a reaction out of proportion to the current situation), see what is beneath it (often a childhood injury), and respond in a different way. If the trigger indeed hearkens back to childhood, you send compassion to that wounded inner child, but you don't fall into the feelings of that child—or not for long. Or you may recognize you have been triggered, but you have the skills to stay in the present and to bracket those feelings.

There will always be the deficits and traumas from your past. They happened. But when you have worked through the pain and made up for them the best you can, you don't have to be at the mercy of them.

Healing as Growth

Healing should not be measured simply by what goes away (unwanted impacts or symptoms), but also by the positives that are added to your life as a result of going through this process. In other words, you should also take into account how much you grow.

Just as the butterfly struggles to release itself from the cocoon, struggle is often an inherent part of growth. Facing pain gives us strength that many who have not been tested or have avoided pain generally do not have. Research into post-traumatic growth has recognized the development of new capacities, new directions in life, better relationship skills, and an improved perception of self. All of these are examples of growing as a person.

There's another benefit we don't often talk about. It comes with a breakthrough to our deeper nature. Rather than be broken, we can be "broken open." When broken, we don't have resilience, so when knocked down, we stay there. But when broken open, we expand. We become deeper and richer, and have more wisdom, clarity, and compassion, all qualities that can be described as more of our soul nature. Our hearts open and embrace more. We perceive and eventually start living from a part of us that has always been there, waiting to be freed. This is a kind of "breakthrough bonus." You not only get out of the cramped cage you've been living in, you find your wings and soar.

2

Tools for Doing the Work

If you are getting the sense that working with mother wounds brings up a lot of emotions, you are absolutely right. Opening your awareness to what your childhood environment was like brings up feelings that were often hidden before. Cultivating a sense of safety and staying within it will help you manage what can otherwise feel overwhelming. We'll start there.

Building a Sense of Safety

A sense of safety is a complex thing, affected greatly by your earliest years. If you didn't feel safe then—perhaps because of dangers in the home or because Mother wasn't a safe haven—you may continue to live in the shadows of that as an adult. When your inner world doesn't feel safe (because of harsh feelings, memories that would be overwhelming if acknowledged, or things you have protected yourself from being aware of), it colors your experience of the outer world as well. Scanning for danger, including internally keeping watch for threats that could erupt from the unconscious, is something you do without even being aware of doing it.

Cultivating a sense of safety is crucial. In this chapter, you'll learn how to create a safe place in your mind as well as in your external environment.

Creating a Safe Place in Your Mind

Perhaps you had a place in your mind you could escape to when things were really bad. If you don't already have one, you can build one. This mental safe place is a place you can retreat to when you're feeling overwhelmed, a place that brings you a sense of comfort and peace. It may be based on a place you've been many times, a place you've seen in photos, or one you invent in your imagination. Perhaps you go there in your dreams. It is a place where you feel safe and may be cared for by others whom you've put there for this very purpose.

One of the easiest, most supportive ways to build your safe place is to let someone guide you in a visualization. This might be done in person, by reading a transcript of a visualization, or by letting an online video take you through the process. (You can find guided videos on YouTube by searching for "safe place," "safe space," or "safe haven.") If you find visualizing easy, you can simply quiet yourself and ask for the right place to come to mind. You might also use art supplies to make a representation of your safe place or look for pictures to incorporate.

Your safe place may be *this-world* based, or it may include otherworldly and magical qualities and beings. You might take a place you found solace in years ago (like a special tree that held you as a child) and adjust it, moving that tree to another location, or adding another element, such as an animal you see as a protector. It is important that your safe place not have any elements that make you feel unsafe, so check for that, and if you find any, consciously replace them.

In building your safe place, you want to bring in as many senses as possible. Listen for the sounds of this place. Take it in with your eyes. Feel the temperature and whatever touches your skin. Notice good smells.

One way to test the effectiveness of your chosen place is to check in with your body's responses. Can your body relax there? Do you breathe more deeply? What tells you this is a safe place?

The more often you visit this safe place, the better established it will become and the stronger a resource it will be for you.

Creating Safety in Your Environment

Working with your safe place is good training for your nervous system and a great emergency backup, but there are also practical elements you can control in your environment that impact how safe you feel. Rather than serve as a refuge from the present (as the safe place in your mind does), these elements are right here in your everyday life and can make it easier for you to stay present.

What makes us feel safe is different for each of us. One person may feel safer with others around, another when alone, and yet another with only their most trusted beings nearby. When I want a safe space to do emotional work, I turn off my phone, sometimes lock my door, and adjust things so my space feels comforting and not distracting.

When you are preparing to do any kind of emotional work that might be dicey, including exercises in this book, you may choose to have some comfort items available. They could be something you hold (a stuffed animal or doll), something that holds you (like a small blanket or shawl), or something intangible like a soothing sound or scent.

As part of feeling safe for delving into a certain exercise, you may consider what kind of support you want available from a safe person. Do you need to have someone with you, someone not physically present but whom you can reach if you need to, someone who will check in with you after a certain period of time, or that you can touch base with later?

You don't want to replay your experience with Mother where you aren't given what you need, so choose your support persons carefully. Some people may want to support you and yet do things that get in the way of your process. For example, they may provide premature reassurance or try to make you feel better rather than simply "holding space" for you to feel exactly as you do. Some get too involved in the content or in problem-solving. Some aren't really up for it, or aren't up for it at that time—even though they said yes.

What Helps You Feel Safe in Your Daily Life?

Let's identify elements in your everyday life that contribute to a feeling of safety. Make a list of as many of these elements as you can think of, and then underline those that seem the most important. Include things like lighting, temperature, sound, smells, and objects within your visual field as well as inner conditions. You don't need to use complete sentences. Here are some examples.

- Having my phone with me
- Being in a familiar setting
- A comfortable ambient temperature
- Thinking of someone I feel connected to
- Taking a moment to connect with myself, including checking in with how I am feeling emotionally and whether I can feel my feet on the ground

_____

_____

_____

_____

After making your list, read through it carefully and use it to create strategies that can help you feel safer when you're likely to encounter distress. For example, if having your phone with you makes you feel safe, you may want to plan to keep it within arms' reach whenever working on the exercises in this book. Or, if warmth is needed, you may want to sit in a sunny window seat or turn up the thermostat.

This exercise is a start, but developing a deep sense of safety is an ongoing project. In chapter 7, you'll learn that emotional neglect and abuse can rise to the level of trauma and leave you with complex PTSD (page 94). A central characteristic of PTSD is that until it is resolved (usually through therapy), your nervous system and unconscious carry a feeling that the trauma is not over—you are still under threat. So, to feel safe, you need to clear the cache, working through what maintains the sense of danger.

If you notice yourself being even slightly on guard, ask yourself, "In this moment, am I safe?" This can help you become more present and perhaps recognize that the only danger right here, right now, is what you are subtly bringing into the situation. You can provide yourself realistic reassurance, like "The door is locked and no one can get in" or "Even if he doesn't like it, he's not going to physically endanger me." You can also call up times that you've felt safe and how that felt in your body, and remind yourself, "I'm safe right now."

You might also think back over your life and recall any times when, in retrospect, you wonder if you were protected by a guardian angel or some other spiritual force, because you can't otherwise explain how you survived. Maybe you are one of the lucky few who has memories of supernatural rescues. You can also work on an energetic level to put up boundaries and even assign sentries to protect your space.

Setting Boundaries for the Work

It helps to create parameters for your inner work so it doesn't disrupt your outer life more than necessary. Although there will always be times when you are triggered and need to sit down with yourself and do some processing, it will help if you intentionally build some times into your life to handle part of the load. The more time you make for processing, the less the pressure will build and then spill out at inopportune times.

What I'm talking about here is building a "container" for the work, just as happens when you go see a counselor. Therapy sessions provide natural boundaries where your emotions may surface, peak, and recede. You can create a container on your own by marking off time to do inner work and creating a safe space. Having a container you can relax into also requires trust—trusting another person or trusting yourself. Some even say, trusting the process—in this case, trusting that you will know what to do and that your psyche is doing its best to work with you.

Developing a partnership with your unconscious is part of this. One day early in my trauma recovery I was out hiking when I felt I was about to have a new memory. That did not feel safe in the middle of nowhere, so I said, "Please wait until I get home." Putting out that simple request worked, and my unconscious held back the memory until I was ready for it. Once you've proven your dedication to doing the work, your unconscious will do this more automatically.

Having Your Feelings without Your Feelings Having You

Over time you'll learn how to support your emotional work without flooding, or being overwhelmed. You are more likely to flood when you lose awareness of the feeling as a feeling and collapse into it. The feeling then becomes everything.

There are a number of tools that help you avoid flooding. One is to take a step back and put some space around it. You zoom out and find the *you* that is feeling the emotion. In doing so, you get bigger than the feeling and can recognize that the feeling is only a feeling. It is not all of you and may not even reflect what's really happening. Mindfulness practices help you learn to stay aware in the moment.

Another technique is to imagine pushing a Pause button. When you pause a scary movie, it helps you remember it's just a movie. It's harder to stop the movie going on in your mind, but it's powerful if you can do that. You can also change perspective deliberately, for example, by asking, "I wonder how [other person] is experiencing this?" or "I wonder what this will feel like down the road?"

Another tool that is always available is to anchor yourself by feeling your feet or points of contact with your chair. Centering your attention in your body pulls the energy away from a spinning mind.

I'd prefer you to work with your emotions in a more calibrated way than the cathartic ways we used back in the 1970s, when people were whaling away on pillows with plastic bats. Catharsis encourages feelings to come out in an unchecked and amplified way. In recent years, particularly in trauma therapy, it has fallen out of favor. One reason is that you may allow your feelings to really "blow" without staying present to feel them. You lose yourself, just like with flooding, although this time you are lost in both the emotions and the actions. I'm not saying you shouldn't cry or make sounds and movements when working through a hard emotion. You might even do some no-holds-barred yelling, but this shouldn't be what you rely on. Rather than losing control as in catharsis, you can use less control, neither clamping down on your feelings nor getting lost in them. You can release emotions naturally when you feel them within a context of safety, with "one foot out" to witness them while staying anchored in your body.

Another thing that you must do to avoid "your feelings having you" is to stop your repetitive thoughts. It is referred to as "looping" when you go over the same territory again and again. When looping, you think the same thoughts and marinate in the same emotions, some of which are harmful. Changing this always involves gaining some control over your thoughts. You can find techniques for stopping unhelpful thoughts in cognitive behavioural therapy, but what I find most helpful is to have enough awareness that I can notice being caught in a loop and change the channel by firmly intending to.

Signs of Trouble

Doing inner work can be destabilizing, so watch for the following signs.

- You find yourself getting especially anxious, depressed, or panicky.
- You find yourself dissociating. When dissociated, you can't think clearly, you don't feel very present in your body, you're numb and not all here. You can't find your eyeglasses when they are right on your head. Dissociation is generally disorienting and uncomfortable, although in fulfilling its role as a circuit breaker (keeping you from even more intolerable states like terror or panic), it may offer a temporary sense of relief.
- You have been so overwhelmed recently that you are not meeting your outer responsibilities.
- You are responding to overwhelming emotions by shutting down. More than just blunting your feelings, you are hiding away in bed, not wanting to do anything.
- Your health is running down. Perhaps you're not eating properly, you are depleting yourself by crying too much (that can happen!), or your sleep has deteriorated.
- Others close to you express worry about you.

If you notice signs of trouble, my advice is to get more help. A psychotherapist trained in family-of-origin issues, who does long-term work, and with whom you feel a good connection will likely be the most helpful. If your psychotherapy does not include guiding you into body awareness, it may be good to find someone trained in one of the bodywork modalities (massage or somatic therapy, for example) who understands the body–mind relationship, and may help you release blocks of tension in the body or help you regulate your emotions using body-based practices. If none of these is available, a support group is another option.

If you are already working with a practitioner, discuss the work you are doing with this book and ask for help in modulating it.

Self-Help Tools for Moments of Overwhelm

When you are overwhelmed, you want to give yourself some exit strategies rather than staying with what is so painful.

Here are five strategies for dealing with dissociation and emotional overwhelm.

1. **Regulate your breathing to help regulate your nervous system.** Begin by noticing your breathing just as it is, and then slow it down by lengthening your exhale. See if you can let the air all the way out, and allow the inhale to start on its own. Trying too hard or thinking you must breathe deeply may backfire, so keep it easy and gentle. We want to befriend the breath and normalize it more than control it. Keeping your tongue pressed against the roof of your mouth helps stimulate a calming response and prevents you from mouth breathing or clenching your jaw.

2. **Move your body consciously to help you get more grounded.** Move slowly and gently and drop your weight into your feet. You can lightly tap on your body or use another kind of touch that feels stabilizing, like placing your hand over your heart. Any of these actions can be paired with reassuring words. If you have a yoga practice, you might try a few asanas that feel stabilizing to you.

3. **Focus on the present and your physical environment.** Notice the colors, sounds, smells, and so forth around you. Pay attention to what it is like *right here, right now*. Often when overwhelmed or dissociating, you are caught somewhere inside, in a different time (decades ago). Tell yourself, "Yes, but that is not happening now."

4. **Give yourself time to "come back" from the work you were doing.** Do something simple like wash the dishes or water the plants. If you have gone into a state of hyperarousal, where you feel hypersensitive and jumpy, it may take twenty minutes, during which you aren't replaying in your mind what is upsetting you, to really settle back down.

5. **Tune in to something that feels good to you—a good memory, a supportive person, perhaps a pet that is right there with you.** You might go to your safe place or incorporate any of the other cues that help you feel safe.

Identifying Strategies You've Found Useful

Take a moment to remind yourself what tools you already have in your arsenal for when you're feeling emotionally out of balance. Make a list of the helpful strategies you've collected over the years, then go through your list and put a star next to your favorites.

_____
_____
_____
_____
_____
_____
_____
_____
_____
_____
_____
_____
_____
_____
_____
_____

You might keep this list handy and treat it as a "cheat sheet" to refer to when in a place that makes it hard to think. It's also good to review this list periodically so you can add new favorites.

Journaling Techniques

Journal writing is a proven method for processing feelings. I use it all the time for my personal healing. Writing helps you stay with your experience (even allowing you to note when your mind is trying to pull you away from it), provides comfort and support similar to what you get from talking with someone, and helps you track what you are moving through. Many of the exercises in this workbook utilize journaling. There are two techniques I like to recommend.

Freestyle writing. This is where you write whatever comes to mind, not following any particular structure. Generally, I journal with a pen, but you may express feelings quite forcefully using crayons or markers or by changing to your non-dominant hand. This helps you decrease mental elaboration and drill down to your more primal feelings.

Dialogues. It is very simple to do dialogues in your journal. You simply go back and forth between two or more perspectives, moving to a new line each time you switch. I like to place a mark or initial in the left margin to signify who is speaking.

You can dialogue with anyone: someone who is alive, no longer alive, or has never been alive (a more archetypal figure). You can also dialogue with parts of yourself, parts of your body, and even situations you find yourself in. Most of the dialoguing called for in this workbook involves either a supportive figure or a supportive part of yourself, and a part that is hurting. If you've done a good amount of therapy, you may have internalized your therapist's voice and be able to respond to your hurting self with what that person would say (or do). When you are really open to your therapist's energy, you will hear some things you don't expect.

Armed with these basic tools, you're ready to get into our primary subject: Mother.

3

Our Need for Mothering

As infants and young children, we cannot survive without mothering. Mothering is a whole set of activities and roles, and any person providing it may be considered a mothering figure. The deepest mother wounds are generally caused by the first mother, either a birth mother or an adoptive mother who takes over soon after birth, but any mothering figure can leave behind wounds. This may be a father, an older sibling, a grandparent, a nanny: all of these might best be considered surrogate or substitute mothers.

Before we begin addressing these wounds, it helps to understand the complexity of mothering, especially the needs Mother fulfills in our first years. Here, I list ten things we need from Mother during these years.

What We Need from Mother

In our first years, we need a mother figure to provide the following.

1. **Safety and protection.** We need a protected enclosure when we first come into the world. A safe haven. This is what Mother should be. In our early years, we need protection from overstimulation (noises that are too loud, lights that are too bright), protection from falling or otherwise hurting ourselves, protection from dangers in the world we haven't yet learned about.

    Without a feeling of safety, all of our resources (limited as they are) are shunted into survival functioning, leaving us with many deficits to make up for later.

2. **A positive experience of attachment.** Being able to "attach" to others by forming an emotional bond is the basis for our entire relational life. When Mother doesn't lay

down the template for this, it makes it harder to form secure attachments to anyone. This bonding also gives us a sense of belonging.

3. **A reliable source of help.** Infants and toddlers are totally dependent on their caregivers, and we learn during these years whether we can expect help or not. If not, we often shut down and stop communicating our needs. As the psychologist Erik Erikson noted, we learn either that we can trust that others will be there for us, or that they will not.

4. **A stand-in for your undeveloped nervous system.** When we are born, we can't regulate our response to upsetting experiences, so we need someone—generally Mother—to stand in for that while we develop this capacity.

5. **Mirroring.** You've likely seen mothers make facial expressions that match what their baby is feeling. This is nonverbal mirroring. Not too much later her words do the same thing, giving names to states and feelings: "You are so tired" or "You are really angry!" or "How strong you are!"

    Important messages come through all of Mother's behaviours and feelings. Does she seem unhappy and far away, or does she light up when she sees us? Mother is constantly communicating to us who we are by signaling who we are *to her*—for example, that we delight her or bother her, are precious or a burden. These messages may never be verbalized, yet we absorb them, and they leave a mark.

6. **Good touch.** Gentle, loving touch is not optional. It is a requirement. We learned decades ago that babies in orphanages who received the least amount of physical holding often didn't make it. As with other cases of failure to thrive, they did not develop normally, and a disproportionate number of them died during infancy.

    On a physiological level, touch does many things; perhaps most important is teaching us how to calm down and get out of stress states. It is an important part of bonding, and without a capacity to bond, we are locked in a cold world. Good touch helps us feel safe, feel present in our bodies, be here. We need Mother to provide the kind of touch that helps us with these things.

7. **Love.** Feeling loved tells us we have value, that we are precious and should be treated well. It is a primary source of nourishment, as important as milk and, later, food.

8. **A secure base.** A secure relationship with Mother gives us the confidence and courage to move out and explore the world as we move toward preschool age. Without this security, we're afraid to venture out. We need to know that Mother is there to return to.

9. **Encouragement.** When Mother encourages and cheerleads us, it provides valuable scaffolding for us to try new things. If we don't have much support, we may become an underachiever or compensate by pushing ourselves in a way that doesn't ultimately serve us.

10. **Mentoring.** Mother figures are our first mentors and teachers. A lack of development (of language, motor skills, relational skills, even of our nervous systems) can result from insufficient stimulation and teaching, especially early in life. A mother guiding us is not the only way we learn, because we are constantly absorbing information from all around us, but having someone patiently and directly helping us is a big advantage. It helps if they teach us in a way that is calibrated to us and that we sense that they want to help us.

So, as you see, mothering is not just providing food and shelter. Mothering is the basis for our foundation, what we could see as the infrastructure of our psyche. Unfortunately, many mothers don't have the skills and capacities to provide this.

How Well Did Your Mother Provide These Functions?

This exercise can help you begin to get a picture of how adequately your mother provided for you.

Most children don't have well-formed experiential memories before the age of four or five, and it is even later for those with more traumatic pasts. You may not have hard data to hang your hat on here, and that's OK. I'm just inviting you to reach for a sense of your experience.

Rate each of the following on a scale from 1 to 3.
1 = I can't remember getting much of this, and my feeling sense is that I didn't.
2 = Mother probably did an adequate job, although I don't know for sure.
3 = I think Mother did a good job with this.

	RATING
Providing nourishing touch	
Helping me not be bandied about by extreme emotions	
Being there in a reliable way, so I knew I could get the help I needed	
Providing a secure relationship for me to rest in	
Giving me a sense of having worth and being lovable	
Providing a feeling of safety and protection	
Providing a secure base	
Guiding, encouraging, and teaching me what I needed to know	

If you rated any a 3, do a little celebration dance. These, along with 2s (adequate), indicate ground and stability in your foundation.

I don't imagine that many reading this book will see ratings that are this high. I've had people tell me they can't get past a 1 on a scale like this. Remember, this is no reflection on you but rather on what you have gone through.

Many mothers do not understand all that mothers should provide. They just followed their own mothers' example, didn't know better, or were too handicapped by their own issues to provide everything you needed. You, in contrast, want to understand mothering, even if it stirs up some grief. You are pursuing a path of growth. Deep bows to you.

Mother Is What We Are Made Of

Mother is where we come from. She is like the ocean we exist within. In the first six to twelve months, we are psychologically merged with Mother. We feel her feelings and respond to much that she is going through. It takes several years for us to fully emerge from that fusion with Mother into a self of our own. Even then, we continue to carry Mother inside of us.

We do this by internalizing Mother. She becomes like an invisible structure within us. If you are well mothered, that structure feels like a layer of support and good feelings that is always available. When you are not well mothered or your mother is not well (doesn't have coherence and solidity in her own structure), you may feel like something is missing in you. Really, that lack is what was missing in Mum.

Mother's sturdiness and her active support are part of what helps us grow our internal structure, but so is how she performs simple everyday tasks. Does she brush your hair and bathe you with gentleness and love, or does she do it in a perfunctory way? Is she attuned to your rhythms and preferences, or do these get lost in her wanting to just "get things done"?

We can say the ways Mother meets your needs are the musical notes of the relationship. Are those clangy, discordant notes or harmonious, comforting notes? These notes are embedded in your nonverbal memory and are not conscious until you take time to reflect on them within a context that helps makes sense of them. Then, from deep in your memory, the feeling tones in the relationship start to percolate. This may happen as you use this workbook. It's good to let them become conscious and articulate them. It brings the relationship into the light.

What Did Your Support Structure Feel Like?

To help you register your first feeling response to your mother, invite up an image from your unconscious using the metaphor of scaffolding. Don't force an image; just wait for one to appear as you relax and hold the questions: What did Mother feel like to me? Could I rely on her? If she were a piece of scaffolding, what would that look like? It might look like the scaffolding on the face of a building or a trellis for a plant. Is it rickety and insecure, or does it have lots of sturdy cross-supports? Is there enough support for you to fully develop, or might it leave you lopsided? How did that support feel to you as a child?

Go ahead and describe the image that comes to you, or make a quick drawing. Then take some time to freewrite about how this scaffolding felt to you.

Your Childhood Home

Although Mother is usually the central figure in a young child's life, she doesn't exist in a vacuum. In fact, the more she abdicates her mothering roles, the more important the surrounding environment becomes. When the family environment is healthy, it helps compensate for weak mothering, and when it is unhealthy, it exacerbates it.

Your childhood home includes everyone who shared the home, how they related to each other, and how the physical home was managed. Ideally, home felt like a safe and stable place. Too often it was not. There are many things that determine whether home felt safe. One is whether there was harmony between those living together or if you had to watch out for sniping and conflicts. These may have broken out between parental figures, parent and child, or among the children who lived there.

Most important is that the home was free from violence—real, threatened, or hidden. Being free of physical violence alone is not enough. Hostility and indifference between family members is also toxic. When treated with indifference, you learn that you don't matter. You may as well be a piece of the furniture. Some flee to other homes or to Nature in hopes of feeling safe and held, but you shouldn't have to do that. Your home is your nest as a child, and the nest should hold you and be comfortable.

In a healthy home you are not walking on eggshells—around anyone. It helps if others aren't walking on eggshells either. When people are too on guard and too careful with each other, there's no room to relax. And relaxation is the basis of health and well-being.

A healthy home feels stable and orderly, at least to some extent. You aren't living in a construction zone or among unpacked boxes. This is not just a stopover. You know whether you can expect meals, and if so, when. There are distinctions between different parts of the house and appropriate boundaries. You can have privacy (and safety) without hiding in your closet. The family (even if a family of only two) comes together at times. Healthy families come together often, sharing many different activities or just hanging out together. In a healthy family, people like and enjoy each other.

A healthy family is a happy family. Naturally there will be unhappy moments, but when there is a complete lack of happy times, it's like living on scorched earth that badly needs rain. It's the good feelings that give us a sense of belonging together.

Characterizing Your Childhood Home

This exercise in characterizing your childhood home may help you make sense of feelings that you have carried about it.

Circle or highlight the words and phrases in each of the following lists that fit with your memory of your childhood home.

LIST 1
- chaotic
- hostile
- uncomfortable
- impersonal
- scary
- crisis-prone
- unsafe
- uncomfortably silent
- felt like a prison
- felt like a train station
- no privacy
- disengaged
- enmeshed
- secretive
- hostilities or animosities among some members

LIST 2
- predictable in a good way
- friendly
- fun
- loving
- respectful
- engaged
- mostly happy
- affectionate
- open
- supportive

Note in which of these lists you circled more words: the first list (negative) or the second (positive). Since things are often not all one way or the other, you may have identified items from both lists.

You may also use this exercise to look at living situations in your adult life. What patterns do you notice in both?

Identifying Your Role in the Family

In this exercise, we'll focus on roles you took on and how you were treated in your family. This is accomplished by stepping outside yourself and describing what others would see.

Take as much space as you want, but write one or two paragraphs at minimum. Use extra paper if needed. Write in the third person, referring to yourself not as I/me but with a name or pronoun. For example, "Johanna was the scapegoat in the family. When she spoke, others laughed or put her down. She was overweight, and sometimes her brother would grab food from her hand. . . ."

_____
_____
_____
_____
_____
_____
_____
_____
_____
_____
_____
_____
_____
_____

This exercise may leave you feeling a little tender, so give yourself time to sit with that. You might go to your journal and write about more memories or feelings that came up during the exercise.

Telling Your Story

The previous exercise was one way of telling your story, but certainly not the only way. More common is to tell it in the first person. You could once again use writing, but here, let's try sharing, whether with an individual partner or a larger group, your experience of growing up.

Sharing your story with others provides you with an opportunity to be "felt." You bring them into the story with you, just like with a novel or movie. You are not just saying, for example, "I was invisible," but describing the actions of others that made you feel invisible. The listeners' verbal feedback and body language tell you that they are feeling it with you. This can be a strong bonding experience.

It's good to lay out some ground rules before beginning. It's common in many groups to use a timer. I'd suggest trying 5 minutes per person. Using a timer doesn't have to mean you are abruptly cut off, as the general rule of thumb is to allow the speaker to finish their last thought. (A timekeeper can also signal when there is just a minute left.) If you feel complete before the timer goes off, just signal that. Sometimes one person's sharing kicks off too much for another person in a group to hold, so if necessary, group members should be able to leave and do some self-support. This isn't ideal, but it may be better than someone acutely uncomfortable in the room distracting from the story the speaker is telling.

When in the listening role, your job is to "hold the space" for the speaker, listening from a place of openheartedness. I suggest keeping any feedback short, such as a single statement of empathy (for example, "I really feel how lonely that was for you"). You want to keep your feedback focused on the person who just shared and try not to turn attention to your own experience. It may be easier to keep these boundaries in a support group or class than when sharing with a partner or small group, where it's tempting to get further involved.

Identifying Allies

If you were lucky, you had allies in your environment. Your ally could have been another mothering figure (a partner of Mother's or a mother down the street), a grandparent, a sibling, or even a pet. Naming someone as an ally doesn't mean they were always a support for you but that they were sometimes there in a way you could count on. Identifying who was there for you can help round out the picture and bring in some bright spots.

Make a list of any allies you had and take a moment to think about how each was important to you.

_____

_____

_____

_____

_____

To take this a step further, pick one or two of these allies and write them a letter, describing how they helped you and thanking them. Use extra paper if necessary. You don't need to send this letter; just writing it has connected you with a valuable resource from your childhood.

_____

_____

_____

_____

_____

_____

If you didn't have anyone who felt like an ally, did you have a favorite place or a belonging that was a comfort to you? Write about that.

_____
_____
_____
_____
_____
_____
_____
_____
_____
_____
_____
_____
_____
_____
_____
_____
_____

We'll continue this exploration of your early environment with a series of exercises in the next chapter.

4

The Mother of Your Childhood

In this chapter, we'll be calling on your childhood memories and impressions of Mother—some of which haven't become conscious before now. We'll also look at how the relationship changed over your childhood years and what happened as you became an adolescent.

This chapter is heavy on exercises. Take whatever time you need to complete them and give time for your new awareness to settle in. You might do only one exercise in a sitting. That's just fine. As you work, remember the tools from chapter 2 (page 21) for processing feelings.

Getting Honest about Mum

Before you dive into this exploration of how you experienced Mother, it's good to recognize at least some of the many (valid) reasons you have for not knowing all of this already.

As a young child, you were totally dependent on Mum and needed to protect the relationship with her. There are two main dynamics involved. The first is that it is too destabilizing for a young child to see Mother as other than good and capable. The analogy I use is that just as you wouldn't want to learn the pilot is drunk or hallucinating while you're on a plane, as a child you don't want to know that Mum is not up to the job. The second is that you needed to contain feelings that could disrupt the relationship—feelings that could come with seeing the situation more clearly. You can't afford to disrupt *her* good feelings toward you, so it's best to bury anything that would do that.

The feelings and awarenesses that would have been disruptive during your early years are still disruptive when you bring them up now. They disrupt the status quo in your relationship, your life story, and your emotions. This disruption is the price of healing what you have not allowed yourself to see before now.

Various "protectors" stand at the door of the unexamined past. Probably the one that looms largest is guilt. Society puts mothers on a pedestal, saying that we owe them for having sacrificed so much for us. To be critical, angry, or ungrateful makes you bad, so it's easier not to look. Psychological defences like minimizing and denial also make it harder to go there, as they are protecting you from the hurt that will come with seeing the whole truth.

Healing your mother wounds begins with getting honest about your experience. Keep in mind that experience is always subjective. The feelings and images that come up now can't be taken as reflecting an objective truth. Young children don't have a nuanced palette of emotions or understanding of the world. Their emotions are more black-and-white and easily changeable. One moment Mother is everything to them, and the next they are screaming, "I hate you!" So it's good to uncover not one but many experiences before drawing conclusions. The exploration in this chapter will include unearthing memories, impressions, and events to help you clarify your image of Mother.

Impressions of Mother

Our first memories are not very filled out, sometimes revolving around just a single image. That may be Mother crying—or waiting endlessly for Mother to come while *you* are crying. It's a snapshot that emerges against a darkened background more than a narrative with context. First memories are believed to reflect an important theme that is carried forward. We generally have very few memories of our first years, and those we do have were important enough to break through.

Uncovering Your First Memories of Mum

In the space provided, describe the images that form the first memory or two that you have of Mum. Because these early memories are not firmly anchored, elements of one memory might combine with another and thus not be true in a literal sense. Don't worry about it. You're just noticing your impressions in this description.

_____
_____
_____
_____
_____
_____
_____
_____
_____
_____
_____
_____
_____
_____
_____

Take a moment to sit with the images and feelings in any memories that came up. Is there a theme you can identify? Keep that theme in mind as we continue. You may want to do some journaling to invite more to come up.

Describing Mother

Let's fill out the picture of Mum. The following is a selection of words that might describe her. Read them and circle those that fit best. If you wish, put an X through any word that you feel is quite the opposite of Mother.

involved	potent	quirky/different
loving	impotent	warm
worn out	dependable	cold
calm	tight/controlled	clueless
harried	tense	perceptive
upset	untrustworthy	distracted
overwhelmed	hateful	self-absorbed
thriving	kind	formal
temperamental	passive	distant
patient	disorganized	critical
wise	isolated	encouraging
frightened	withdrawn	exhausted
mean	mechanical	emotional
immature	generous	intrusive
angry	depressed	hard to reach
not there	anxious	insubstantial
"motherly"	conventional	unreliable

Now that you are warmed up, you may think of more words or phrases not in this list. Write them here.

_____

_____

_____

_____

_____

_____

_____

Read through the words you've chosen and write a couple of sentences about the overall impression they leave you with. Stay with yourself as you do this, noting what is hardest to acknowledge and being aware of the counterproductive protectors we talked about. You are piercing through those protections to reach your truth.

_____

_____

_____

_____

_____

_____

_____

Uncovering Your Unconscious Impression of Mum

Putting your impressions into words can be helpful, but it's also good to acknowledge the nonverbal experience that lives beneath your conscious awareness. With this exercise, we'll try to reach around your conscious mind and get a more primal feeling for how you experienced Mum.

Imagine your mother as a room in a building. Now put yourself inside that room. I suggest you do this without deliberation, unconcerned with whether it's your childhood self or your current self. You don't need to have a picture of yourself. Just focus on what it feels like to be in this room.

I expect you will get an immediate emotional "hit." If you can, remain there and let the feeling evolve and reveal more. If that first hit was all you could take, that's fine, too.

Now, write a few phrases that describe the experience. Please don't judge whatever your experience is. It may be a little jolting, unpleasant, or even toxic, but respect it as feeling-level input.

_____

_____

_____

_____

_____

_____

_____

_____

_____

_____

_____

_____

Stepping Stones in Your Childhood Relationship with Mum

Relationships are shaped by events, and this exercise is a chance to identify significant events that happened between you and Mum.

The term stepping stones was used by the psychologist Ira Progoff to refer to formative life events. This exercise's structure comes from his intensive journal method, which is meant to help you get the most out of your journaling by building on your own work.

In the space that follows, make a list of eight to twelve events that feel significant to your relationship with Mum. It's fine to write in an abbreviated form, such as, "The time I didn't want to go to kindergarten without Mum and she pushed me out the door and locked it." Events may be more thematic than discrete; for example, you might name periods when a certain dynamic was present: "Mum was dating Jake and no longer had time for me."

Keep in mind that any time you make a list, it reflects the experiences that are most significant to you right then. At another time, in another mood, you will make a different list.

Letting these markers come to mind is the core of any stepping-stone exercise, so rather than thinking too hard about them, let yourself fall into a quiet, receptive state and then simply write down what comes to mind.

After writing a stepping-stone list, Progoff recommended reading through it and then doing some freestyle writing. What does the list bring to your awareness?

Your Relationship with Mum Beyond Early Childhood

As you grew beyond early childhood, your relationship with Mum changed in a number of ways. If Mother didn't really like the dependency and the 24-7 on-call nature of caring for a small child, she might have relaxed a little as you became an older child or teen. She may have engaged more or wanted you around more, especially if she experienced you as a support. If she was withdrawn or busy with other things, on the other hand, she may have been relieved to have you off on your own.

Although you may have begun expressing your will in primitive ways in early childhood (like insisting on the blue cup rather than any other color), new choices arise as you get older and develop your own ideas, some of which run counter to Mother's. In a more verbal family, you might have had scuffles over these differences, but if you were used to accommodating Mother, you more likely ended up hiding what she didn't like. You may have felt that you couldn't defy expectations, even if they had never been spelled out. If so, that left you living in an invisible cage.

With a really disengaged mother, it may have felt like there was no mother there—never a protective wing around you, but also no one to push up against. Children develop strength by taking a stand for themselves, but there is no taking a stand when Mother is that disengaged.

During the later childhood years your mother may have been reacting to things you could not see. Parents are often triggered when their children are going through life stages that were hard for them. For example, if Mother feels she became a sex object after entering puberty, she may have become anxious and rigidly protective when her daughter entered puberty, or she may have gone numb and or pushed her daughter into situations like those she was put in.

The point is that Mother's reactions to your developmental steps had many contributors. They are not all about you. Nothing from your childhood is all (or only) about you.

Unpacking Your Relationship with Mum as an Older Child and Adolescent

Here are some questions for you to reflect on as you explore how your relationship with Mum changed as you grew older, but before you became an adult.

Was there an age at which you noticed a negative change in your relationship with Mum? If so, what was going on externally at the time (divorce, moving, changes in the family structure) and what do you suspect was going on within her? How did this affect you?

_____
_____
_____
_____
_____
_____
_____
_____
_____
_____
_____
_____
_____
_____
_____

Was there an age at which things got better between you? What do you attribute that to?

Were you eager to become your own person? Were there struggles around that? For example, did Mother react to personal choices about your appearance, giving signals about what was OK and not OK? What happened as you were experimenting with your identity?

Did you feel supported during your adolescent years? What would you have liked more of? What would you have liked less of?

Were you given new roles in the family? (These are often gender related.) Were these comfortable for you? What feelings do you have about them?

Telling the Story of Your Childhood

It can be very healing to have others "feel with you" what you've been through, and sharing your story with a supportive group or exercise partner is a good way to do this. I suggest you each take five or six minutes to share; use a timer as explained on page 32. If you're working in a group of more than six to eight people, you may need to spill over to another session for everyone to get a turn.

Rather than have a preset order for sharing, I like to have group members signal when they are ready to take a turn. What most often happens is people feel ready to go after resonating with the story another person just shared.

If you aren't the one speaking, your job is to receive what is being shared and wait until the end to respond—and only if the speaker *wants* feedback. It's perfectly fine if you don't want feedback. I would limit responses to something very short, just a minute or two, and use the timer here, too. Be aware in giving feedback to stay with the person who just shared rather than turn the attention to you. It's easy to show that you relate by using a knowing, sympathetic look or a short phrase like, "I know that one." The response might include a hug or some kind of touch, but only with permission.

You can also tell your story in your own way to a sympathetic friend or two. They don't have to have their own experience to share, but there tends to be more camaraderie when you are doing this with others who are also on their own healing journey.

I wanted you to have some time opening yourself to your own experience before you moved on to the next chapter, which looks at what constitutes an emotionally absent mother. This way, you aren't simply primed to see certain things. You're ready now to take the next step.

5

Emotionally Absent and Emotionally Abusive Mothers

Now that you've been bringing up some experiences with Mother, let's examine whether she fits the description of an emotionally absent mother, an emotionally abusive mother, or both.

What Is an Emotionally Absent Mother?

Being an emotionally absent mother isn't all or nothing. It falls on a continuum. Your mother may have shown some but not all of the features I describe and will likely have some of these characteristics more than others. I put this description together after interviewing many adults who felt under-mothered, and I have continued to find confirmation for it from clients and readers as time goes on. Here are the central characteristics of emotionally absent mothers.

First, you don't feel Mother as emotionally present. She doesn't seem attuned to your feelings or respond to you in an empathic way. She may have been busy performing other household or work duties, but you didn't have the sense that you were important enough for her to want to attend to your needs.

It's not just that she wasn't attuned to you. If you look closely, you'll find that she was often not very engaged with her own emotions. This frequently presents as a flatter affect, as depression often does, making these mums feel more mechanical than real. Yet it is important to understand that what is underdeveloped is the ability to *tolerate* emotions, and this can show up as being emotionally volatile as well.

We could say that these emotionally absent mothers are "not the mothering type." It may be that they felt they had no option but to have children, as that was ingrained as a woman's role.

Or it may be they had children because their partners really wanted to or because of unplanned pregnancy. It also may be that they wanted (or thought they wanted) children but mothering just didn't come that naturally to them. They may have been happier doing something else, and indeed they may have put more energy into their work life than into their family.

It would be a mistake to think they do not want to be good mothers. They often don't have an internal reference point for good mothering because they didn't experience it as a child. In some cases, these mothers are simply too overwhelmed. Raising several small children feels chaotic to them, or it may be that something is going on in their personal lives that reduces their bandwidth. These same women may show up better when they have grandchildren, which is a different relationship with different responsibilities.

Emotionally absent mothers don't really know their kids. They don't know who their children's friends are, who they like and don't like, or what their children are worried about because they don't ask. Listening to a really involved mother interact with her children might be rather shocking for them.

It's not only that they don't talk to their children much; they also don't touch much. They don't show affection freely. And they are less likely to join a child in activities.

Emotionally absent mothers tend to perform poorly in the mothering roles such as providing protection and supervision and acting as cheerleaders and safety nets. When their children come to them needing help, they often do not respond skillfully, either minimizing or denying the problems, or leaving it to the child to figure out. They don't know their children well enough or have the skill to help them navigate challenges in a calibrated and attuned way. Children often have the sense Mum doesn't want to be bothered, and so they learn not to share their troubles.

It was a revelation when I realized that parents like these don't really like the innate characteristics of a young child. They would rather their children were beyond the messiness and neediness of early childhood. What they reinforce with their mothering—if anything—is that the child should outgrow being a child! The irony is that it is easier to outgrow needs that have been met than to precociously push past them.

When there is not a strong early bond to build on, it doesn't tend to get better in adolescence. Mother's emotional and practical support tends to be misattuned. She may buy you clothes or sporting gear that aren't "you," and her advice or attempted empathy likewise miss the mark. Or perhaps she pushes you to socialize with kids you wouldn't pick or pushes you into activities she thinks you like but you don't.

When you understand how unprepared these mothers are to take on the enormous job of mothering, how unable they are to access the natural maternal instincts that nature provides, you may feel a bit sorry for them.

How Emotionally Absent Was Your Mother?

Make an *X* next to or draw a line through each of the following statements you *disagree* with.

I remember many instances as a child of feeling emotionally close to my mother.

I felt that my mother knew what was going on in my life and was there for me.

My mum's gifts to me were almost always just what I wanted.

My mother was a confidante, and I found her advice very helpful.

My mother had my back and was there when I needed her.

My mother let me know she was proud of me.

I felt like my mother loved being a mother.

It was easy to express affection for, and receive affection from, my mother.

My mother made time to do things with me beyond the bare necessities.

After any kind of rupture between us, like a fight or misunderstanding, my mother would make sure I knew she cared about me, and would apologize if she had behaved badly.

Disagreeing with any of these statements indicates some degree of emotional distance, with more disagreement suggesting greater emotional absence on Mother's part.

Be gentle with yourself here. It can be sad to see that your mother was frequently absent, but it can also be a relief to acknowledge it: "So *this* is what was wrong!" It's cold comfort, but let me say that you were not alone.

Is Emotional Abuse Different?

Emotional abuse is different from emotional absence. Emotionally abusive mothers show some of the same behaviours, but what leads to the behaviours is different.

The main distinction I see is that emotional abuse causes harm intentionally, whereas the neglect of an emotionally absent mother does not. Take, for example, a child screaming for help or crying hysterically. If Mother hears it and feels angry and does not respond because she doesn't want to be at the beck and call of her child, that is abuse. If Mother feels overwhelmed, doesn't know what to do, and tries to distract herself with something else, that is a lack of capacity. She is running from something she cannot deal with.

Abusive mothers seem wired to need to hurt others. It's possible that their biting comments and withholding happen reflexively and are not as intentional as I am suggesting. Perhaps they cannot control their impulse to sting another. The emotionally absent mother doesn't have that impulse.

Let's take another issue, abandonment, and parse the differences. Emotional neglect inherently involves an abandonment of children. Mother is not there to provide what is needed. She may not be physically there and is unaware that she needs to be (for example, she's off on a trip, leaving her four-year-old for two months), although more often she is physically present but not emotionally so. She is, as I've said elsewhere, "missing in action," but she does not intend to abandon her child. Abusive mothers, on the other hand, use abandonment or the threat of abandonment to punish or control. It's effective, since physical abandonment is traumatizing for a young child, threatening their survival. Saying something like, "Keep acting like that and I'll take you to the orphanage" is abusive, as are the nonverbal behaviours of walking away from a child who is in great need or purposefully withholding care.

Emotionally abusive behaviours are, in a word, mean. Emotional abuse is expressed in words that are ridiculing, humiliating, shaming, and blaming. It is expressed in facial expressions, body language, and actions that communicate disrespect or hostility. Abusive behaviours are meant to hurt.

Identifying Signs of Abuse

Just as the previous exercise helped answer the question of whether your mother was emotionally absent, this list is meant to help you determine whether there was also emotional abuse at play.

Make a check mark next to any of the following items that are true for you.

_____ My mother humiliated me in front of others.

_____ I could never be enough or "right" for my mother. She let me know that.

_____ When I needed help, my mother refused to give it.

_____ My mother would get in the way of other family or community members who cared about me. It's like she wanted to isolate me from love.

_____ My mother seemed to compete with me—and always needed to win.

_____ My mother used to threaten to send me away.

_____ If I expressed things I felt good about, my mother would roll her eyes or somehow show I was bad for bragging or that perhaps I was exaggerating or being untruthful.

_____ My mother put me in situations that were not safe, and I don't think it was just accidental.

_____ My mother denied me the things (appropriate clothing, for example) that would keep my peers from mocking or bullying me.

_____ My mother rejected my love for her. She demeaned me when I was affectionate.

_____ The things my mother said made me feel like she hated me.

_____ My mother consistently put her needs before my own. It was as if my purpose was to serve her.

____ My mother was controlling and seldom let me make my own choices.

____ My mother put me down a lot, making me feel unworthy.

____ My mother would sometimes give me the "silent treatment" for days.

____ My mother could be sarcastic and "cut to the quick."

Some of these behaviours seem more over the top than others, but they share a common quality.

Sometimes people defend Mother from accusations that she is abusive by saying it didn't happen that often, that she was drinking or out of her mind, or that she wasn't doing it on purpose. Or they bring up that she is very wounded herself and perhaps was treated in a similar way. You may let the awareness of her wound inform your understanding, but please don't use it to discount the harm.

The basic components of healing set out in this book (facing the truth, working with feelings, understanding why Mother behaved as she did, learning to take in nourishment, and protecting yourself now) will be helpful if your mother was abusive, but you may want to supplement your work here with other material on emotional abuse.

If this is the first time you are identifying that you experienced emotional abuse, I hope you can hold yourself in compassion.

Can Mother Be Both Emotionally Absent and Emotionally Abusive?

Absolutely. If we define emotional absence as not being emotionally connected with and tuned in to a child, you can see that it is like a precondition for emotional abuse. It *allows* such abuse to take place. The abusive mother doesn't hurt when her child hurts and is free to be the agent of such hurt.

But emotional absence and abuse don't have to go hand in hand. As noted previously, Mother can be emotionally flattened or disengaged, or with blind spots related to her own unexamined wounds, and not have this aggressive impulse.

Parsing Mother's Tendency Toward Absence and Abuse

Make a check mark next to the statement that best fits your mother.

____ She fits many of the characteristics of an emotionally absent mother, without abusive behaviours.

____ She was emotionally absent, with infrequent instances of abusive behaviours that I think she felt bad about.

____ She fits both descriptions strongly.

____ She was primarily abusive and not really emotionally disengaged. She is more volatile and knows me well.

____ She was more emotionally abusive than emotionally absent, but also (similar to a battering spouse) could shower me with love.

If you can describe her better using your own words, go ahead and do that here.

_____
_____
_____
_____
_____
_____
_____
_____
_____

Write a paragraph about how you feel after thinking about the previous statements.

_____

_____

_____

_____

_____

_____

_____

_____

_____

Reasons Mother Was Compromised

There are a great many factors that can compromise Mother. Some of these will be more associated with an emotionally absent mother, some with an abusive mother, and some with both. Let's start with those that tilt a mother toward being neglectful but not abusive.

- ☐ She was emotionally shut down, most often because of trauma, grief, or depression. This may have been ongoing or may have happened during a critical period for mother-child bonding, such as soon after giving birth. Maybe she has lived at a distance from her emotions all her life.
- ☐ She was emotionally immature, stuck perhaps at an adolescent level—or earlier. That makes her way too young to mother well. This lack of development can also be present in her cognitive and social skills.
- ☐ She was preoccupied with herself, either because of immaturity or narcissism or because she wasn't in a secure place. This could be due to her current circumstances (her other relationships, financial resources, and so on) or to something like unresolved trauma, which always left her focused on her own survival.

- ☐ She knew almost nothing about parenting and hadn't taken the time to learn.
- ☐ She was a single mum—or functioning as one. There was too much to do and too much responsibility for her capacity.
- ☐ She experienced overwhelming insecurity, perhaps due to famine, war, or poverty. This left her preoccupied, worried, and struggling to survive.
- ☐ She was busy taking care of someone else, such as an ill parent, spouse, or child.
- ☐ Being a career woman or working too many jobs left her without energy when she came home.
- ☐ She had wounds around bonding that prevented her from trying to bond.
- ☐ She spent too much of her energy trying to protect herself from an abusive partner or perhaps to protect you from that partner's rage, making you hostages together.
- ☐ She didn't have the physical or emotional endurance needed to parent well.

Now let's name some factors likely to contribute to being emotionally abusive.

- ☐ She was scarred by being emotionally or physically abused herself.
- ☐ She has a mental illness.
- ☐ She holds a lot of hate and anger inside.
- ☐ She is acting out her hate on you. Perhaps you remind her of someone.
- ☐ She has poor impulse control.
- ☐ She is very fragmented inside.
- ☐ An addiction had her in its grasp.
- ☐ She learned really bad parenting behaviours from her own parents.

The last two items could be on both lists, and I'm sure other factors we could bring in would be, too. Let's remember that difficult circumstances affect us all differently.

What Compromised Your Mother?

Return to the previous two bulleted lists and make a check mark next to the items that may have compromised your mother. You may be guessing at some, and that's fine. Then take some time to think about what was happening for your mother during the time you were growing up and list any additional compromising factors that come to mind here.

Now read back over all of the factors you identified, and then write about how it affects you to acknowledge them. Does it in any way change how you think of Mother?

The Mother You Lived With

This exercise utilizes everything covered in this chapter to this point. It is a chance to share with your group what kind of mother you lived with. Was she emotionally absent, abusive, or both? Use the material on what compromises Mother if that helps you create a picture of her.

Have each person take 5 minutes to talk about their mother. Do not provide immediate feedback. After everyone who wants to speak has spoken, go around the circle and share as few as a couple of words or as many as a few sentences about how you feel hearing about what everyone has lived with ("I'm saddened at how much neglect we all went through, and I find myself angered when I hear of people I care about treated abusively" or "I feel quiet and internal, but also closer to you all.")

See if anyone has a suggestion for ending the group with something uplifting. That could be a prayer, a poem, hugs, or any kind of affirmation. Let it come from the group as a felt response to the moment.

Why Might You Feel Under-Mothered While Your Sibling Does Not?

Sometimes, the same woman, in other circumstances or with a different child, functions as a better mother. That doesn't help you, and it may even make her under-mothering of you feel worse. It feeds into the natural tendency of a child to fall into the trap of thinking "It must be because of me."

There are many reasons why you might feel under-mothered while a sibling of yours does not.

1. **Circumstances.** A child who doesn't come home from the hospital for some time, has medical problems, or is a "difficult baby" for any reason at all affects the relationship between mother and child. The method of birth also matters: Mothers who have cesarean births take longer to attach. Certainly, something like post-partum depression makes a big difference, as does a mother's readiness for a child. I've known of first children of young mothers (especially when those children are the result of accidental pregnancy) who are not mothered nearly as well as later children who may come with marriage, more stability, and maturity.

   The list on pages 58 to 59 contains a whole raft of circumstances that significantly make Mother less available. These circumstances show up at different ages for siblings, with early ages generally more affected by Mother's unavailability.

2. **Individual differences.** This relates to the uniqueness of each child but also to how good a match that child is with Mother. Children with a sensitive temperament (this is inborn) often register Mother's slights and shortcomings more than do more laid-back children with hardier constitutions. Emotionally absent mothers will be at a greater loss at how to deal with a more sensitive child.

   Moreover, a child who reminds Mother of someone she has issues with (a parent, sibling, significant other, or herself), in either appearance or personality, may be unconsciously treated differently. Mother will be more comfortable with some children than others. Maybe it's the one who doesn't like to cuddle—or who does.

3. **Gender.** Mothers often treat boys and girls differently. Some of this relates to sex-role stereotyping, and some to Mother's own history. She may be more comfortable with one sex or the other. She may value female children less, or have an idealized mother-daughter image she wanted to live out.

   A mother may be less aware of treating her children differently than the kids are. As a child, you may have been subtly aware of biases, but it may be only as an adult that you understand this. Preferences may, for the most part, be hidden—although often there are unexplainable feelings buried inside. One example is the sense that "Mummy would have liked me better if I had been a boy."

What Impacted Your Early Relationship with Mum?

Use these questions to help you explore your relationship with Mother. You can't expect to know your mother's psychology fully, so just answer as best you can.

Were there circumstances related to your birth that may have contributed to less-than-ideal early bonding?

_____
_____
_____
_____
_____
_____
_____
_____

What other circumstances of your early years may have caused your mother to be less resourced or available to you?

_____
_____
_____
_____
_____
_____
_____

How similar or dissimilar are you to your mother temperamentally? Can you think of anything in your appearance, temperament, or needs that may have been hard for Mum? Are there perhaps ways you reminded her of parts of herself that she rejected? These may include situational similarities; for example, she was molested by her father and so were you.

Did Mother seem to have a preference around gender? Have you since noticed any patterns that suggest this?

Healing Old Resentments with a Sibling

Learning about the many factors that shape a mother-child relationship may help you understand why a sibling had a different experience than you did. As a child, you couldn't parse it like this and may have felt jealous or resentful of the easier or more privileged relationship another child had with Mum. It also may be, as in the second example that follows, not that the sibling had a favored position, but that their needs affected what Mum had left to give to you.

This exercise is meant to help you acknowledge feelings toward a sibling who seemed to get more than you did and to see if there is anything now that might help you. You can do this exercise with more than one sibling in mind, but always one at a time.

In the space that follows, write out what you'd like to say to your sibling, imagining that you are speaking to them in a more direct way than usual. Include as many of the following as you can.

- A reason this sibling had advantages with Mum or how they affected what Mum had to give you
- A feeling you have now or had as a child that is related to that (including a feeling about yourself)
- Anything that would help you resolve this with your sibling

Here are two examples.

1. Mum liked you best. That's how it always felt to me. I think it's because you were like her in some ways that I am not. Both of you like a lot of attention and are very involved with appearance, and I'm a more introverted, intellectual type. I felt quite isolated and unseen. I don't really expect to be close to you, but I wish you would at least acknowledge me as part of the family.

2. I don't know all of what was going on with you. You were so defiant and got in so much trouble that it wore Mum out. There was no role for me but Good Girl and Mum's Helper. That had real costs for me, as it has taken my whole lifetime to know my own mind and make *me* important, too. I resent how your behaviour impacted the family.

In some cases, there may not be something you can identify that would help, and in other cases there may be: You want that sibling to acknowledge something or to understand your experience or possibly even to apologize if they mistreated you.

After writing what you would express in a more candid conversation, you may decide to go ahead and communicate this with your sibling if you feel up to that and believe your sibling can hear you. (If you expect hostility, you might choose to let it go or share your work with someone who can be supportive.) Just giving yourself permission to feel your grievance is often the first step in working through it.

In this chapter we've focused on the *what* (emotional absence and emotional abuse) and *why*. The next chapters will help you identify how all of this impacted you, and how you can begin to heal from it.

6

The Impacts of Being Under-Mothered

As young children, we are like soft clay, easily shaped by our environment. If we grow up with love and attunement and other good mothering qualities, it leaves us with many assets. If we do not—if we are under-mothered—we are left with unwanted impacts.

It's important to keep in mind that various factors can leave the same kind of mark, so we can't say with certainty what caused a particular effect. For example, if you have trouble trusting people, that may come from your parents' having been totally unreliable, or from a significant betrayal in adulthood. What we're doing here is looking at impacts that *might* come from early emotional neglect or abuse.

> ### How Does Your Legacy of Being Under-Mothered Show Up?

Make a check mark next to the items that have applied to you at some point in your adulthood, even if they no longer apply. You're looking at your legacy here, the burden handed down to you. You may notice opposite items on this list; this is because the same cause can have opposite effects on different people.

____ I have trouble warming up to people and trusting them.

____ I feel confused when people are nice to me.

____ I have carried a sense of not being lovable.

____ For a long time, I felt that no one really knew me—and it's taken time to know myself.

____ I don't have a lot of self-confidence or self-esteem.

____ I often feel insecure and wonder if I am enough.

____ I am afraid of failing.

____ I'm indecisive and don't feel confident in my ability to make good decisions.

____ I am not comfortable expressing my emotional needs.

____ Sometimes I feel starved for love.

____ Romantic partners have described me as closed off and self-protective.

____ Romantic partners have described me as clingy and insecure.

____ I often feel lonely and alone in the world.

____ I have had to learn how to receive help, affection, or compliments from others. It doesn't come easily for me.

____ I have often hidden my feelings from others.

____ Life feels like a struggle for me. I don't expect things to go well or to have abundance, either material abundance or an abundance of friends, fun, love.

____ I have struggled with depression, anxiety, or other mental health symptoms.

____ I often eat to self-soothe.

____ I have had an eating disorder.

____ I have been addicted to alcohol or drugs or things like sex, work, or exercise.

____ When someone wants me, I have a hard time saying no. I need to be wanted.

The Impacts of Being Under-Mothered

____ I don't ask for much from people, including at work.

____ I hadn't always recognized it, but I show signs of not feeling safe. I spend more time than necessary in a hypervigilant state, on the lookout for danger. I'm not sure I ever completely relax.

____ I have a blind spot and don't recognize when a situation is not safe.

____ I think I have to be perfect to be loved.

____ I have a strong inner critic.

____ It is not easy to express myself authentically and spontaneously.

____ I don't take good care of my health or do nice things for my body.

____ I don't seem that connected to my body. I'm tangled up in my mind and emotions and often don't recognize that I need to move or drink or use the bathroom.

____ I am highly sensitive in terms of sensory inputs and get overstimulated easily.

____ I seem to sabotage myself when I'm about to succeed at something big.

____ I sometimes feel not really here.

____ I can't remember much about my childhood.

____ I am far more sensitive to criticism and rejection than I'd like to be.

____ I push myself in ways that my mother pushed me and rarely do anything to pamper myself.

____ I feel empty inside.

____ I often miss "attachment cues," signals that someone wants to be close. For example, an acquaintance asked me if I liked going to movies and I didn't think until later that she was looking for a way to spend time with me. I also notice that I don't keep eye contact or return a smile easily.

____ I get involved with partners who don't treat me well.

There can be reasons other than under-mothering for these characteristics, but good mothering would have prevented most of them. For example, if you were always treated with respect growing up and easily got your needs met, you would likely not get involved or stay with people who badly mistreat you. Use this exercise as a mirror to point out possible connections.

As you can see, there are numerous ways that under-mothering can show up: in your feelings about self, your attachment patterns, your comfort with or need for touch, and your struggles in life, whether they be with moods, confidence, or achievement. You may want to reread the overview in the introduction, and *The Emotionally Absent Mother* covers this topic in even more detail.

I focus on the psychological impacts, but body and mind are deeply intertwined. The findings of a major study—the Adverse Childhood Experiences, or ACE, study—document that those with more adverse circumstances in childhood suffer with more health problems later in life. With these major life stressors, your nervous system and immune system, in particular, get off to a rockier start; these contribute in countless ways to various disease states. These effects and their mechanisms are detailed in the book *Childhood Disrupted* by the science writer Donna Jackson Nakazawa.

Emotional Bonding

Your first experience of bonding was with a mothering figure. Early bonding with a caregiver is largely determined by how that person meets your needs, by their eye contact and touch, by a synchronized dance between you, and by their expressions of love.

If you didn't bond with your mother or another caretaker or family member, developing a strong, durable bond with others may be challenging. Sometimes it comes when you have a child, but we know that's not guaranteed. It's not uncommon that people bond with pets before they graduate to bonding with other people. Some people never develop strong emotional attachments or bonds.

That doesn't mean there is nothing connecting you with a particular person. Rather than a bond built on safety and love, we can be tethered to others with strong feelings like obligation, resentment, frustration, conflict, even hate. There's a kind of bonding that happens when people go through intense experiences together, like a disaster or a significant death, as well as when they find a joint purpose or cause. I'm distinguishing this from emotional bonding formed by positive feelings of attachment and care.

Exploring Your Bond with Mum

Let's apply this understanding of bonding to your relationship with your mother. The exercise on page 64, What Impacted Your Early Relationship with Mum?, started us on this subject, but here we'll extend it a little further. Following each prompt, write a little about what you see.

On a scale of 1 to 5, with 5 being a very strong positive bond, how would you rate your first five years with Mum? Can you identify a feeling quality to that bond? Can you give an image to it?

_____
_____
_____
_____
_____
_____
_____
_____
_____
_____
_____
_____

At what point in your childhood or adolescence did you feel closest to Mum? If you can't think of a time, write about how that feels for you.

What do you think your bond was made of? Previously, I made the point that we can be glued to someone by negative feelings, and certainly by circumstances. Name as many feelings as you can that tethered you to Mum. Note whether the bond feels like an asset overall or has more negative characteristics.

Do you feel positively bonded with Mum now, and if so, what contributed to that?

Sharing Your Bonding Experience

Sharing vulnerable topics like this strengthens a group bond. You can also share with a listening partner who is not on this journey.

Before sharing this aloud, work through the prompts in the previous exercise. Then take turns (3 to 5 minutes each) sharing with the group what you discovered. After each person's sharing, make time for a brief but heartfelt response, remembering the guidelines given on page 32.

Your Experience with Emotional Bonds

Let's look at how your bonding experience has gone. We want to acknowledge both what has helped and what has hurt you in relationships. First, we'll list those that you have bonded most closely with (pets as well as people). Then we'll identify what most facilitated that bonding and what limited it. For example, someone being very solicitous and generous may have facilitated bonding, but then an instance where trust was broken limited it.

Significant losses, depending on such particulars as your age, can leave you hesitant and self-protective, not wanting to love and lose again. Examples include the loss of an early attachment figure (through death or moving outside your orbit), the painful breakup of a romantic relationship, or the loss of a best friend or significant mentor.

In each space that follows, name an important relationship in your life, then complete each of the sentence starters. Repeat for other important relationships, using extra paper if necessary.

Name: _____

We got close when _____

It helped to have someone _____

Our relationship changed when _____

The gift of this relationship was _____

Name: _____

We got close when _____

It helped to have someone _____

Our relationship changed when _____

The gift of this relationship was _____

Name: _____

We got close when _____

It helped to have someone _____

Our relationship changed when _____

The gift of this relationship was _____

After writing about each of these important relationships, write about how your bonding experiences have affected you.

_____
_____
_____
_____
_____
_____
_____
_____
_____
_____

Needs and Dependency

Naturally, if your needs were not well met as a child and your dependency was rejected, there will be things for you to work through so that you can allow yourself to show needs or have any dependency in later relationships.

Our default settings on this are correlated with the attachment style we first had with Mother. Some people with mother wounds feel helplessly dependent or amplify their dependency to get their needs met (a more anxious, clinging attachment style), while others refuse to let themselves become dependent (an avoidant, self-sufficient attachment style). You can move beyond these insecure attachment patterns, but it takes work.

If you're fortunate to spend time in a healing relationship (with a partner, therapist, or any close person), you may learn to have what is called an *earned secure attachment*. From there we don't need to deny needs or use them to hold others hostage, because we've learned to trust someone to be there for us. (See page 113 for more about learning to trust.)

Identifying How You Feel about Your Needs

Make a check mark next to any of the following statements that express how you feel about having emotional needs that become obvious in a relationship. You may check multiple items.

____ 1. Needs are inconvenient. They are an opportunity to be hurt.

____ 2. If I show my needs, people will run the other way.

____ 3. I often get my needs met, and that feels good.

____ 4. I see what I can provide for myself first before going to another with a need.

____ 5. I've been hurt too many times to divulge my deeper emotional needs.

____ 6. My partner is *supposed* to meet my emotional needs. I get mad when they don't.

____ 7. Partners are supposed to meet emotional needs?!

____ 8. I'm the one meeting others' needs.

If you checked item 3, you may have had a secure relationship in childhood or had an "earned secure" attachment later in your life. This takes away the charge around expressing your needs. Items 1, 2, 4, 5, and 7 are more indicative of a self-sufficient style. Item 6 describes the more anxious style, possibly even indicating that you're trying to extract from a partner a consistency that was absent with Mum. And item 8 is more like the caretaker attachment style. You can learn more about all of these attachment styles and their connections with Mum's behaviour in *The Emotionally Absent Mother*.

What Might Allow You to Need Another?

This exercise gives you a chance to compare where you are with where you'd like to be in terms of allowing yourself to need another person. It also helps you identify what limits you. If you cannot let others be there for you, it will make healing much harder.

With the left end of the following line signifying no tolerance for dependency and the right end signifying total comfort and even a positive expectation of your needs being met by someone else, draw an X on the line where you would place yourself right now. Draw an O at the place where you would like to be.

Now, write about what is getting in your way. Is it lack of trust, self-protection, fear, unfamiliarity, not wanting to be a burden, feeling you don't know how to communicate skillfully, or something else? See if you can name the factors that you'd need to work on to become more comfortable.

_____

_____

_____

_____

_____

_____

_____

_____

_____

Your Experience of Touch

After the medical situations related to your birth, your first experience with touch is generally with your primary caregiver, usually Mother. We can think of this as establishing your touch "settings." These determine how you respond to touch in various situations. The settings can change, but that takes learning and doesn't happen immediately.

Emotionally absent mothers tend not to touch their children much. Touch, after all, is a form of connection and emotional bonding, and this is what they are not so good at. Everyone receives some touch, as it is baked in to various parenting tasks. How that touch is experienced is very important. Touch can be mechanical, cold, or harsh, leaving you not wanting to be touched. Just as Mother's facial expressions are a reflection of how she feels about you, her touch mirrors the same.

Touch also helps you locate yourself in your body rather than feel disconnected from it. Good touch coaxes you into relationships with others. If you don't receive enough touch, it may leave you feeling untouchable (even if not consciously so).

Touch is an essential nutrient, and you'll suffer if you don't get enough. It can leave you with elevated stress hormones and a nervous system that tips more often into the fight-or-flight response. Lack of touch can stunt the development of your immune system. It also sets into motion patterns that have consequences for your relationships. You may turn off your need for touch, become *touch aversive* (in which receiving touch feels uncomfortable), or feel an insatiable touch hunger that can drive you into the wrong places.

> ## Identifying Your Feelings about Touch

Make a check mark next to each of the items that are more true for you than not.

____ I enjoy being touched, even by people I don't know well (as long as it is good touch).

____ Even though I enjoy touch, it does not feel natural to me to initiate touch (except when I have been drinking or am in an altered state).

____ If someone touches me in a nice way, I get a bit dysregulated (feel ungrounded, excited, off balance, or emotionally charged).

____ I generally don't like being touched.

____ I've had to learn to accept touch in my intimate relationships. It was not easy at first.

____ Generally, being touched does not feel safe to me.

____ I hunger for touch but do not show it.

Uncovering Your Touch History

Knowing your touch history helps you connect the feelings you identified previously with where they may have come from. Answer each of these questions as best you can.

Make a list of the major people in your early childhood environment, including all caregivers, and next to each, write a few words about how you remember touch with them. Use extra paper if necessary.

What did you notice about how your mother touched others, such as other children, partners, or friends? Did Mother seem to enjoy touch? What did she want or not want from you in terms of touch?

What kind of touch do you remember in your early school environment?

What kind of touch do you remember in your adolescence?

_____
_____
_____
_____
_____
_____
_____
_____
_____

Make a list of your romantic relationships and for each choose a few words that describe your experience of touch.

_____
_____
_____
_____
_____
_____
_____
_____
_____
_____

Were there incidents of abusive touch? From whom? How frequently?

Have you been comfortable providing nurturing touch to children, elders, or friends?

What do you notice about how you touch your own body? Is it with care and affection? Do you rarely touch your body except in functional ways? How does this reflect the way your mother touched your body?

_____

_____

_____

_____

The previous exercise may stir up uncomfortable feelings, so take a moment to notice what is happening inside and ask yourself what would feel good. Doing something that feels good (that is not, in the long run, self-harming) is a way not to let negative feelings take over. In order not to keep ruminating over the same content, you need to interrupt the pattern you are in, by turning your attention to something absorbing or to a positive state where you feel comforted.

How You Treat Yourself

We're going to talk about self-care again in chapter 12 (page 169), but here we will look at connections between how you treat yourself and how you were treated. Here are some patterns you might see.

- If you internalized hostility from a parent, you are prone to treating yourself harshly and using a lot of critical self-talk (see page 169 for an introduction to self-talk).
- If you had a more neutral but checked-out mother, you are more likely to be unintentionally neglectful of your body, emotions, comforts, and needs.
- If your mother was a mess and you needed to take care of her, you might continue to put others' needs above your own.
- If Mother acted as if you didn't deserve to be here, you might engage in self-harming or high-risk behaviours that could lead to serious injury or death.
- If Mother acted as if you couldn't do anything right, you might treat yourself as a dummy who can't do anything right. Notice I don't say you will, but you are more likely to see yourself this way. That's partly because of how self-concept forms and partly due to copying the modeling of Mother.

Do You Treat Yourself as Mother Treated You?

Now let's try to spot any correlations in your life. On each of the following lines, with the right side as the positive side, make an X for where Mother was in this behaviour and an O where you put yourself. Do the best you can, understanding that you cannot know what she sees and feels, only what she shows you.

Attending to my body as if it is precious

Valuing and supporting my intellect

Seeing my creative talent

Willing to spend money on me

Recognizing my individuality

Seeing me as someone others would be lucky to know

Honouring my preferences

Proactively supporting my health

Being generous with me

―――――――――――――――――――――――

Being generous with praise

―――――――――――――――――――――――

Showing concern for my safety

―――――――――――――――――――――――

Showing enthusiasm about my accomplishments

―――――――――――――――――――――――

Being nurturing toward me

―――――――――――――――――――――――

Where your Xs and Os are close together indicate areas where you follow Mother's lead. You might compare these with areas where the Xs and Os are far apart. What would you say is responsible for the difference?

Now, go back and draw a star on each of the lines to indicate where you would *like* to be. This will help point you to the things you may want to work on.

The first stage of healing is all about recognizing what happened and how it affected you. It's hard work, but it's a necessary step in freeing you of some of the baggage you've been carrying. As the author John Bradshaw said, what you thought were your personal *defects* can now be understood as *deficits* in your childhood upbringing. Seeing the bigger picture relieves you of taking the blame on yourself.

7

Trauma and Triggers

Looking at trauma will broaden the lens that we have been using to look at your experiences. We don't always think about childhood emotional neglect and abuse as *traumatic* or as overlapping with other kinds of trauma, but they do.

In this chapter, we'll dig into trauma, spend some time with self-rejecting feelings, then go into an exploration of triggers—what they are in general, what your relational triggers are in particular, and how to limit your reactivity to them.

What Is Trauma?

The term *trauma* is used to describe situations that are overwhelming and outside your control. They shake you to your bones, leaving you wondering if you can survive intact. Technically, the term *trauma* refers to the *reaction* to these events rather than the events themselves, but most people refer to the events as trauma, and I do that as well.

Some traumatizing events are easily recognized (war, assault, disasters), while others go under the radar because they are more common. The kind of emotional neglect and abuse described in the previous two chapters is significant enough to be considered trauma. In fact, emotional abuse and severe neglect are right up at the top of the list of most harmful situations. (Notice your reaction while reading this.) The events involved may be small, everyday things, but their impact is big.

Let me explain a few more terms.

> *Attachment trauma* comes from an attachment figure, such as a parent, who is unavailable or inconsistent. For example, a mother being absent for months before a small child

can tolerate that can have long-lasting traumatic effects, as does a mother who is right there but is mis-attuned or unable to provide the care the child needs.

Complex trauma (also referred to as *complex PTSD*) generally stems from repeated experiences in childhood that generate fear, helplessness, and instability, including abuse and severe neglect. You may also find it called *developmental trauma* or Developmental Trauma Disorder (DTD).

Don't worry too much about which words to use. I offer this more as validation that these are recognized kinds of trauma.

Conditions Related to Trauma

Unresolved trauma can lead to depression, anxiety, panic attacks, eating disorders and other addictions, emotional numbing, chronic tension in the body, and medical problems that seem to defy explanation or treatment, especially those involving chronic pain and autoimmune disorders.

The condition we most often associate with trauma is post-traumatic stress disorder (PTSD), which we'll take a moment to dig in to. You can have PTSD *and* any of the other conditions just named.

PTSD is characterized by symptoms that cause significant disruption to normal life. Here are the three major categories of symptoms.

1. **Reexperiencing the trauma.** If you have PTSD, one of the ways you suffer is that you keep reexperiencing the trauma in some way, such as distressing memories, dreams, or flashbacks. Overreacting to things that remind you of the trauma is also considered reexperiencing, even though you may not be aware of what you are reacting to. We'll cover this on page 100, in the section "Triggers Point to Your Wounded Places."

2. **Avoiding reminders of your trauma.** Not being able to get beyond the trauma is so distressing that you naturally want to avoid anything that may remind you of it. Most of this is unconscious, like not understanding that you don't eat meals at a table because it brings up uncomfortable feelings from the dinner table as a child. The essence of trauma is feeling trapped, so keep this in mind when you think about avoidance. Numbing yourself can also be an avoidance, such as through addiction.

3. **Increased arousal level.** Unresolved trauma keeps your nervous system in a state of heightened arousal that can result in a number of symptoms like startling easily, hypervigilance, feeling irritable and reactive, and having difficulty sleeping at night or

concentrating during the day. You may also experience physical symptoms, such as rapid breathing or heart rate.

Complex PTSD involves all of these symptoms and a few more. Those frequently named are as follows.

- Difficulty controlling or "regulating" emotions
- A negative view of yourself with the self-rejecting emotions described in the following
- Difficulties in personal relationships
- Challenges to your "systems of meaning" (you may not feel that you live in a safe and good world, for example, or that there is hope for humanity)

The trauma caused by our attachment figures leaves deep impressions, both because we are younger and haven't yet built a foundation and because these are coming from people who are supposed to be taking care of us, thus there is a betrayal involved. Not feeling safe is sometimes tagged as a major characteristic of complex trauma, but you see it in the hypervigilance of all PTSD.

Whether you develop PTSD is a matter of many factors, most of them outside your control (so don't blame yourself). These include the following.

- How old you were when the traumatic event occurred
- The amount of previous stress
- Your psychological hardiness before the traumatic event
- How your nervous system is wired, what kind of innate sensitivity you have
- The nature of the traumatic stressor (some events lead to PTSD more often than others; when we are personally targeted—especially by someone we know and depend on—it more likely leads to PTSD than impersonal traumas like a natural disaster)
- Whether you had any control in the traumatic event(s) and could do anything to help yourself or others.
- The amount and quality of social support available after the trauma
- Appropriate intervention after the traumatic event or when symptoms appear

When you look at this last list, it will make even more sense that the kinds of injuries we are talking about in this book are more likely than others to lead to PTSD. Remember that you can have some of these symptoms but not to the degree that qualifies as PTSD, or you could have had enough distress to be diagnosed earlier but not now. Also, there can be a lag of years before these symptoms reach the level recognized as PTSD. You might, for example, have had a traumatizing childhood, a somewhat normal adolescence, and then become overwhelmed by trauma symptoms in your thirties or forties. This may be the result of a stressor that parallels the original trauma or a pileup of stressors that surpasses your resources for coping.

If it's important to you to know whether you have PTSD, you could go to a clinician for a diagnosis. (C-PTSD is not yet part of the diagnostic system used by many US providers.)

Diagnosing a problem can bring clarity and sometimes relief, but you can also become overidentified with a diagnosis, which can distort your experience of yourself. Remember, you are so much more than any conditions you are diagnosed with and so much more than what happened to you.

Changing Frames

Just as we recognize that changing the frame on a picture can have significant impact, applying a different framework to your challenges yields a different view. Let's see how moving to this new framework affects you. Answer the following questions as best you can.

Did you ever consider that you may have experienced trauma or have a trauma disorder? How does it feel to apply this framework to the history you've been working with? What new insights and questions come from learning about trauma?

_____

_____

_____

_____

_____

_____

Is there a reason you do not want to use the label "trauma"? If so, what is that reason?

_____
_____
_____
_____
_____
_____
_____
_____
_____
_____
_____
_____

Feelings of Self-Rejection

Perhaps you can see why it is hard to emerge from complex trauma without feelings of self-rejection. These are most baked in when there is any kind of abuse—physical, sexual, or emotional. But just having your open, innocent self actively rejected or treated with indifference can lead to these, too.

I see this as a family of related emotions: self-criticism, unworthiness, shame (the feeling of being inherently bad), self-rejection, self-loathing, and self-hate.

Everyone is self-critical at times. Most people feel unworthy, at least in certain situations. When these feelings are there much or most of the time, they may interfere with our relationships and our happiness. The emotions I am calling out go above and beyond these more universal feelings to the far end of the list—shame, self-loathing, and self-hatred. Entire books have been written about *shame*, and if the word resonates with you, I encourage you to look up some of them. I'm going to focus on self-hatred.

Self-hatred is sometimes understood as your hatred toward another that you cannot allow so you turn it against yourself, or hatred *from* another that you internalize and continue.

One way this balled-up energy comes out is through intrusive thoughts and images. They are labeled "intrusive" because they are just that—they intrude in an unwanted manner, often startling and disgusting you. Intrusive thoughts and images are not uncommon in people who have PTSD. Often these thoughts and images are aggressive in nature and appear out of the blue. An example is suddenly imagining doing bodily harm to another, usually to an innocent person standing in for your own innocent self who was victimized. It's important to see this as an expression of this hateful energy and not really you.

Feeling hatred hardens you—to yourself, to others, to anything loving that comes your way. Before you can get to taking in love, this hateful energy will need to be cleared. How?

You can start by searching for any self-rejection or self-hate and feel into when it first arose, where you hold it in your body, and where it may come from. You weren't born with it, so it comes from somewhere. If you can see that it doesn't really belong to you, that you absorbed it from someone else, that can help you begin to disentangle from it.

Self-hatred may also be the result of blaming yourself for something—probably falsely. It may help if you can become aware of what you are blaming yourself for and get more objective. Unjustly blaming yourself may include hating yourself for being a victim. It's important to see you weren't the one doing wrong and you didn't have the power to stop it.

Another good antidote for any kind of self-loathing comes when you go deep enough to recognize the real you. If you can feel your essential goodness and innocence, hatred can't cling to you. It clings to you because you see yourself as fundamentally other than this.

Searching for Signs of Self-Hate

Let's search for any shards of self-hatred you may carry by using sentence stems. Finish each with the first response that comes to mind.

If I hate myself for anything at all, it is _____

_____

What brings up the most hatred in me is when I see _____

_____

If I hated anything or anyone as a young child, it was _____

_____

I sometimes have intrusive thoughts of _____

_____

I can't understand why I _____

_____

When I am mistreated in any way, I generally blame _____

_____

Please don't reject yourself for having negative energies cling to you. Keeping them under wraps can actually maintain them, so it is good to make some space and acknowledge them. You might review the tools we talked about in chapter 2 for not collapsing into feelings (page 17). Also, getting more support is always an option.

Triggers Point to Your Wounded Places

A *trigger* is anything that prompts a larger-than-called-for emotional reaction. It is actually a link to a former experience. The more charged the former experience, the bigger the charge when that is stimulated now. Triggers can range from situations that leave us uncomfortable to ones that leave us terrified.

It's common to talk about sensory triggers. The war veteran reacting to a car backfiring is one example. But triggers don't always rely on a sensory channel. Often, what links two situations is how we felt. It may be that the doctor that you've had for a long time moves out of the area while you are in a challenging health situation and suddenly you are in a vulnerable position with no one to trust. You now get a double dose of the feeling—what is arising simply from the current situation along with the emotional charge lingering from the original situation.

Another example is being dependent and unable to get the attention you need to resolve a critical issue. That happened recently for me with a tech company whose help I am dependent upon. The clue that I was responding to something more than just the present was how desperate I felt. By tracking my feelings, I realized they relate to being in a life-threatening situation as a child and not being able to get anyone to listen.

The more traumas and really painful experiences you've had, the more triggers are likely to be there. On the other hand, the more healing you've done, the less likely triggers are to do more than tweak you in the moment.

The confusing thing about triggers is that you feel undone by something, perhaps feeling overwhelmed, helpless, desperate, frozen, collapsed, or enraged, and yet you don't know why it is hitting you that hard. The triggering event itself shouldn't derail you this badly. But the trigger points to what did derail you that badly. You just don't see where the trigger is pointing.

To recognize something as a trigger requires that you consider that there is more than the current situation at play. It's all too easy to get into a rant about the current situation, which will keep the feelings and the emotional charge going but without resolving anything. One method that can help you uncover where your reaction is coming from is to write or talk about the theme of the triggering situation. Is this about betrayal? Being overpowered? Total insensitivity to you?

Identifying Relational Triggers

Use this exercise to help you identify things that happen in your current relationships that *might* be traced back to your mother. We'll start by identifying triggers and then ask if they may originate with Mother.

Think about the kinds of situations in current relationships that really undo you. These may happen with a boss, partner, friend, or coworker. For example, it could be when another is a no-show, or when you do not feel considered in decisions, or when someone acts like you are not there. Make a list of these upsetting things in the space that follows. For each, ask yourself, "Is this what it felt like with Mother?"

_____

_____

_____

_____

_____

_____

_____

_____

_____

_____

_____

_____

When you recognize what these events set off for you, rather than being left with a double dose of upset, you can work on a "double solution"—practicing self-nurturance around the deeper original wound and then having more resources available to problem-solve or work through the top (immediate) layer.

Repeated Triggers Can Ensnare You

When a trigger shows up again and again in a relationship, it can not only pull you into a younger, wounded you but also catch you up in a *schema*. A schema is an organizing perception. It shapes how you view and feel about a situation or person, creating more of a one-dimensional caricature. When caught in a schema, you make that organizing perception your reality.

Let me give you an example. If the previous exercise was successful, you have found at least one pattern in current relationships that harkens back to Mother. It may be one primary trigger or multiple triggers in a given relationship that "capture" you so that you no longer see the current situation for what it is. This often happens in intimate relationships when your partner reminds you of a parent, and with bosses or anyone in a position of power over you. Caught in the schema, you no longer see this person for who they are but as a "repeat offender" from your childhood.

So, for example, if you are in a schema about someone who controlled you and overrode your wishes, you interpret everything they do as having this intention and you can't see how they are helping you or care about you. Or if you perceive a friend as being uncomfortable with your intensity and you felt "too much" for your mother, you may distance yourself from your friend rather than look at what might really be going on; for example, there could be situational factors at play or you misinterpreted their behaviour.

The concept of schemas is just another way of looking at how you are distorting the present. Schemas are not always negative, but I am using them here to point out filters that have negative consequences.

As you can imagine, getting out of a schema is a bit like the escape artist Harry Houdini trying to disentangle himself from his bindings. Before you can disentangle a fused image, you need to see that you are confusing two people.

Extricating Mum's Image from Another

If you recognize the dynamic I have described, this exercise is for you. With someone you've tangled up in your mind with your image of Mother, follow these steps.

1. Write about what this person does that brings up earlier reactions that remind you of Mother (for example, they often ignore it when you share something about your feelings). There are probably several things, so name as many as you can think of.

_____

_____

_____

_____

_____

_____

_____

_____

_____

_____

_____

_____

_____

_____

2. Take a moment to feel what your body is reflecting to you when you think of this person. Do you feel hardened, contracted, collapsed? What is the overall effect?

3. Understanding that you have conflated this person with your earlier experience of Mother, make a list of the ways this person is different from Mother. See if you can bring in some characteristics you appreciate about this person that you've lost sight of.

___

Notice how you feel now, both emotionally and physically.

You can abbreviate this exercise for future use. The most important element is to bring in the differences. This helps extract the current relationship from the relationship with Mum.

The next chapter offers a number of exercises to help you extract *yourself* from the expectations Mother put on you.

8

Claiming What Was Lost to You

As you see, when you are under-mothered or treated abusively, you start out with less than you need and with barriers to being who you really are and having what should be yours. It is as if some things have been stolen from you. One example is trust, which I devote the second part of this chapter to. You should have been able to trust that you would be protected and taken care of, and trust others to have your best interests at heart. Bits of yourself were stolen when you had to be a certain way to get the parenting you needed. We'll start there.

Reclaiming What You Changed for Mum

As a child, you are shaped and you shape yourself according to the needs of your environment. The most significant feature of that environment is generally Mother. You are dependent on Mother, so to make that relationship as secure as you can, you conform to what you believe she wants. You both add to and subtract from yourself to fit better with her. The following exercises explore this territory.

What You Added for Mum

First, let's identify what you thought Mum wanted and what you took on in response to that.

In retrospect, how do you think your mother wanted you to be as a child? What would have been the perfect fit for her? These qualities were likely not verbalized as such, but you knew—or tried your best to guess. Did she want children that she could show off? Children who could take care of her? Children to help her with the tasks of parenting? Children who mirrored and thus confirmed her traits? Write this out in the space that follows, being as complete as you can. You can write it as a paragraph or a list.

Now let's look at what you did to accommodate her. Using the previous material to generate a pool of possibilities, but not limiting yourself to those, look at what you took on for the sake of an easier relationship with Mum. For example, maybe Mother wanted you to be well liked and popular, so you became a people pleaser. Also include here ways that you copied Mother's way of being in the world. Maybe she was always busy being productive, and you learned to do that, too. Make a list of what you took on for Mum.

_____

_____

_____

_____

_____

_____

_____

_____

You may like some of these traits and dislike others. It's now your choice. Go back to your list and draw a heart symbol next to the traits you want to keep and an X next to those you do not. The invitation here is to allow yourself to let go of what you took on for Mother's sake—if you choose to.

Here is an example. Denny's mum wanted him to be in sports and to look and act in ways she considered masculine. He adapted to this, because what else is a kid to do?—and because the pressure to fit this mold started so young. Once he left home, he quit sports, let his hair grow, and started studying music.

    Changes like this occur over time and aren't going to be accomplished by doing an exercise in a workbook. What I'm hoping is that this exercise will help you become more aware of what you put on—like a costume—for Mum, and to begin the process of giving yourself a choice about that.

What You Subtracted for Mum

Now we'll look at what you cut off or muted for Mum's sake.

Name at least five things that you believed would be unacceptable to Mother and that you muted to stay in Mum's good graces. Examples may include being more uncontained (even silly), taking up more of the air space in a group, and changing your appearance in ways Mother would never approve of.

_____

_____

_____

_____

_____

_____

_____

_____

_____

_____

_____

_____

_____

_____

_____

_____

Reclaiming a Quality You Muted for Mum

Select one of the qualities from the previous list that you would like to fully own, integrating it into your present self. Try it on over a few days, sharing your intention with a supportive person if you want. These are qualities that have not gotten support, so playfulness, encouragement, and visibility are all good choices.

You might even create a nickname to support this new energy. If your name is Sally and you want to reclaim your right to full expression, you might call yourself Sassy Sally. If you've muted your power, you might use the nickname King Kong to remind yourself that you can be big and powerful.

After giving yourself some opportunities to try on this quality, return here to answer the following questions. If you experimented with more than one change, use extra paper to repeat this exercise for each one.

How are you doing with claiming this quality you want to add?

_____

_____

_____

_____

_____

_____

_____

_____

_____

_____

_____

If it's been a rough go or you can't quite get yourself started, what do you think is getting in the way (self-consciousness, an ingrained sense that it is not acceptable, habit . . .)?

___

How does making this change (or even contemplating making it) affect your feeling about yourself?

___

Making changes takes effort and rehearsing new behaviours, so you may need to create a structure to support you. That might be taking an assertiveness class, teaching a class if you've never done that, taking a leadership position, or joining a group to learn public speaking or a dance class where you get a little wild. You might also turn to your supportive person for help; for example, if you want to practice showing your excitement and being more expressive or even off-color, they might provide an audience for that. Where are your edges (the new things that bring the most growth)? This is unmuting.

Getting Personalized Support

When working to reclaim a quality you muted, it can help to get group support to create a "corrective experience." Corrective experiences help make up for what was missing or harmful in the past. They are also called "reparative experiences."

Although you can do this with just one other person, it will be more powerful if there are several people. In a group, you can each take a turn using a format like this: "I muted my [liveliness, opinions, expressiveness, power . . .] to be more acceptable to Mother. Is it OK if I don't do that here?"

Each group member should then respond to the speaker, one at a time. For example, if the sharer reported muting their opinions, you might say, "I really value your opinions. I *want* to know what you think and feel." Rather than repeating one standard response, respond in a way that is natural and spontaneous for you.

If you meet regularly, you might briefly report back the next time you are together.

If you can add back what you subtracted for Mum, and take away what you put on that is not your natural you, it is a big step toward reclaiming a larger, more authentic you.

Trust

When your earliest caregivers were not attuned to your needs, you will likely have a deficit of trust.

It may be difficult for you to know when to trust and when not to. For example, with a history of neglect and/or abuse, you may be so hungry for affection that you are swept off your feet by people who take advantage. That would be trusting before trust is earned. On the other hand, you might feel mistrustful when people are acting generous toward you, and you wonder, "What do they want?" This may lead to your not being open to the support, warmth, or even practical help being sincerely offered.

I remember a woman telling me she would trust her husband with her life, but she wouldn't trust him with her pocketbook. That's the story I want you to use as a guideline because it shows the discernment required. It's a question of trust with what? Under what conditions? To say it another way, trust is not all or nothing. I have learned that I can't trust a number of friends to do what they say they will do. Does that mean they are dishonest or manipulative people? No. Often they have an awful memory or can't carry through with anything without being distracted.

Trust is also relevant with people we go to for help. I'm thinking of two of my health care providers: With both I trust their intentions, but with one, I trust her knowledge base more.

Assessing Trustworthiness

We want both our trust and mistrust to be based on experience rather than an immovable default. Where we'll have the most problems is where we've been most deeply injured in the past. Where there are wounds, you are most likely to do the following.

- Project onto others, filling in what was true in the past
- Emotionally shut down and no longer be able to think critically or use your intuition
- Prematurely trust, because you haven't learned to calibrate or discern trust

For example, the deepest injury in my life (my sexual abuse) was being used solely for someone else's benefit. I am thus sensitive to others imposing their agenda on me. If you've grown up with an emotionally absent mother, a common challenge is trusting someone to be there, to show up, to care about you. If you had an abusive parent, the challenge may be to know whether you can trust people not to intentionally hurt you. (Anyone can hurt you unintentionally.)

Knowing Your Vulnerabilities

With those previous examples fresh in your mind, identify where your vulnerabilities lie. When is it hard for you to trust or to calibrate your trust rather than simply fold and have no standards or be rigidly closed to trusting?

In other words, when does it feel too vulnerable to be open and flexible? Is it when people seem to be pleading with you, when they automatically expect certain things, when you haven't known someone long? Is it when people are probing, and you don't feel permission to tell them to back off? When you love someone? When is it hardest to trust? Use the space that follows to name what you can see in yourself.

_____

_____

_____

_____

_____

_____

_____

_____

_____

_____

Do your responses tend more toward mistrust, premature or misplaced trust, or perhaps cautious trust?

Mapping Areas of Trustworthiness

Now pick a particular person in your life. Write their name or nickname and break down where they're most and least trustworthy. As well as areas like sex, money, confidentiality, include capacities like the following.

- Using good judgment
- Being self-aware
- Having honourable intentions
- Being honest

Where I can trust _____   Where I can't trust _____

Repeat this exercise as needed for different people.

You're probably seeing that for most of the people in your life, there are some things you can trust them with and others you can't. This is OK: What's important is knowing which is which.

Building Trust

Building trust is a matter of several things.

- Learning when you can trust your intuition, feelings, and judgments (all different)
- Gaining experience with a specific person so you have some data to go on
- Taking calibrated risks

We have to take risks to gain experience. How else will you know if a person can hold your vulnerable feelings or sensitive information? The trick is to risk some, but not too much. Not where it could really set you back. Loaning your car to someone you don't fully trust may be a practical risk you don't want to take. There are emotional risks too, like sharing something that is too big, too vulnerable to put out there and have it questioned, ridiculed, or ignored.

The Power of One Trustworthy Person

You can sometimes overcome a lifetime of mistrust through an experience with just one trustworthy person. If you feel you have had a mold-breaking experience, name the person who provided that for you in the lines that follow. What was it that helped you make this monumental shift? Were they honest to the core? Sensitive enough to know where not to step? Loving in a way that was new and corrective for you? If you've had this experience with more than one person, do this exercise for each.

Perhaps you haven't had an experience like this. Not everyone has. For you, I offer this exercise in the hopes of your seeing the possibility. A friend of mine told me of the woman who, by loving her unconditionally, showed her that she is lovable and taught her to open and accept love. This left her more open to trusting that it can be safe to let someone in.

_____

_____

_____

_____

9

The Deeper Emotional Work

Healing is hard emotional work; there is no way around it. It takes time and can be inconvenient. It may feel embarrassing to experience emotions you've kept out of sight for all or most of your life. Hatred is a good example. It helps when you realize how normal it is for a child to feel hatred when frustrated.

The task is to learn to tolerate a wider and wider range of emotions at increasing levels of intensity without losing your balance. It helps when you can stop collapsing into feelings and keep more awareness (page 17).

The emotions that come up in this work will likely be the feelings you held back as a child. You held them back for a number of reasons: because you had no one to help you hold them, to protect a relationship, or maybe because you repressed them right away—an involuntary response. Especially with trauma, we repress feelings.

It is important to remember that feelings are subjective. You can honour feelings as what you felt (or feel now), but you should understand that it's better not to use them to define what happened. You can feel unloved, but the other person may actually love you and be unable to show it. You can feel rejected when others may not be rejecting you. The guiding rule is "Don't believe everything you feel." That doesn't make your feelings invalid.

What all feelings want is for you to meet them. Meet them like you are meeting a small child who is upset. When soothing a child, you don't necessarily join them in their interpretation of the situation, but you empathize with their feelings and reassure them. Emotions need to be felt before they recede. They are like young children who won't quiet down until they've been heard.

Some feelings you may never understand. Emotions can get disconnected (dissociated) from their moorings, and then it's hard to connect them with anything known. Some originate in a preverbal period before you had a mind that could put things into language. What that leaves you with are only the effects of an event (emotions and sensations) and not what happened. It is challenging to work with intense emotionality you can't pin down; sometimes the best you can do is stop demanding to know more.

The Place of Anger

Have you ever met a young child who never got angry? No, because anger is the natural response to frustration. In many homes, Mother doesn't handle that very well, and if your relationship with her was insecure, you may have learned to turn off your anger to protect your fragile bond with her. You may also turn off your anger in an attempt to protect yourself from anger coming back at you from Mother.

I can pretty much guarantee that in the process of opening up your past, anger will come up. It's a matter of giving yourself permission. Feeling anger—and even the rage of your two-year-old self—doesn't make you bad. It just makes you normal.

What you do with that anger is what makes it healthy or unhealthy. It's healthy to recognize and allow anger to come out in safe ways. This may be in a therapy session or a session of inner work you do by yourself, using your journal perhaps, or a judicious use of catharsis. This out-front anger is healthier for you than simmering bitterness or repressed anger, which can lead to depression.

It is most appropriate to deal with this anger without directly involving Mother. There may be a time when you can have a conversation with her about your anger, or an in-the-moment boundary you need to set, but the mother you are most furious with is no longer here. It is the mother of your childhood, the mother in those infant and toddler years who did not come and could not soothe you. (The exercises in chapter 4 help you recall that mother.)

Spending too much time in anger is not good for you. It can become a habit, and you can get stuck in a self-reinforcing loop where the discharge of anger feels like a relief. The goal is to feel the anger without getting caught in a story that will keep it going and to release it in safe, clean ways that can help reduce your store of it. Anger is often a gateway to other qualities and emotions that you'll want to attend to, such as power that you have repressed, sadness, even feelings of love that are blocked. We need to move through that gateway to "get to the goods."

I would say anger is a place we find ourselves in the middle third of the healing journey. It abates as we work through some of it, as we understand Mother more, and as we move into the taking-in, nourishing stage of healing rather than the uncovering, facing-hard-truths stage. I'm speaking in broad terms here; getting too linear about the healing journey would be misleading. You can take in nourishment at any point, and you can feel anger at any point.

Anger lifts as you deal with it. You might start the journey weighed down with depression, which lifts as you begin to allow yourself to be angry, go through some hot days of rage, and end your healing journey with your anger pretty much gone. When others validate your anger, it helps you take what you can from it and move on.

What's Wrong with Feeling Angry at Mum?

Let's flesh out the reasons you hold your anger in by using a repeating question (asking and answering one question again and again). Why would we do that? Because there are always many contributors to a situation, and the repeating question allows us to get at more of them than if we answer it just once. Each time the question is asked, aim for just one response, not a monologue. It's OK to repeat, to pause and reflect, or to just fire back with responses that often come quite rapidly.

Write the question and respond to it in the lines that follow, using a new line for each response.

Alternatively, you can do this with a partner, having them ask you the question for a set amount of time (I suggest at least 5 minutes) without commenting on your answers beyond saying "Thank you," if that feels good.

Here is a question to start with: *What's wrong with feeling angry at Mum?*

_____

_____

_____

_____

_____

Another way you can get to similar territory is to ask, *What might happen if I allow myself to feel angry with Mum?*

I love these "what might happen" questions because they allow you to see what you fear will happen as well as the good that could come from asking them. Try this one a few times.

_____
_____
_____
_____
_____
_____
_____
_____
_____
_____
_____
_____
_____
_____
_____
_____
_____
_____
_____

Feel free to make up and explore additional questions.

Listing Your Resentments

This exercise will help you become more aware of childhood resentments you are holding on to. These will be things you feel angry or hurt about, such as things you feel you should have received from Mother but didn't. You can continue your responses outside the workbook if you wish.

Finish the following sentences, including specific incidents as well as general resentments. Add and fill in more of your own sentence starters if you like.

I resent _____

_____

I resent _____

_____

I resent _____

_____

I resent _____

_____

I resent _____

_____

I resent _____

_____

I resent _____

_____

I wish you had _____

_____

I wish you had _____

_____

I wish you had _____

_____

I wish you had _____

_____

I wish you had _____

Sharing Your Resentments

A group can be a good place to share resentments. Many will be familiar to other members, and this can be validating.

Although I encourage you to have constructed your list ahead of time, you might modify items slightly. You can easily omit names and make those items into something anyone might relate to. Instead of saying, "I resent that you didn't let me spend time with Mrs. Rodriguez," you could say, "I resent that you didn't let me get close to someone who could have provided me with some of the nurturing you did not."

Each person should share only one resentment at a time, so that it can sink in and be responded to. Depending on the size of the group and the time you have available, go around the group multiple times. After each resentment is spoken, others can affirm it by saying something like "Amen!" or "Yes!"

This last step is for in-person groups. After you have all shared as many resentments as you want to (or when time for this is up), make space for an optional group yell. (Someone may need to lead this.) It might be an angry scream or a roar, and it is acceptable to use a few words. This is simply an energetic discharge which can feel good to share. Before disbanding, check in and debrief so that no one is left in the middle of something destabilizing.

Shifting Your Resentments

Resentments, like all feelings, need to be metabolized, which means broken down and integrated. We metabolize resentments by using both validation and understanding.

Go through the resentments you came up with on page 123 and for each item, empathize with the part of you that holds the resentment. You can write this down, but it may be slightly more effective if you say it out loud. Since these resentments are from your childhood, you will empathize with your inner child, saying something like, "Of course you wanted that" or "That made you so mad."

Then explain to the child why the reality was the way it was. You might say something like, "Your mother should have provided that for you, but she didn't know to do that. I'm so sorry." It's not that we are telling our inner child not to feel these resentments as much as helping them see the context they could not see as a child. In doing so, we boost their understanding and validate their experience.

This is too long a process to do here, so I suggest working through it in a journal.

Confronting Grief

One of the things that may surprise you about dealing with your mother wound is how much heartbreak and grief are there. It can feel bottomless.

Grief is not a single feeling but rather a process that involves many of the following feelings: shock, sadness, loneliness, heartbreak, missing what was lost, and anger. As we move through all of this, we may or may not reach a stage of acceptance.

Grief is a natural process that follows loss. Here, it is the loss of what could and should have been there—the loss of a happy childhood, the loss of the security, confidence, and all the other things you might have had in better circumstances. Let's see what this involves for you.

Naming Your Losses

This exercise helps you see the particular losses behind your grief. In the space that follows, list what was missing from your childhood environment. Here are some examples:

- I missed having a parent who was home when I returned from school.
- I missed having a mother who read me stories before bed.
- I missed having a mother who could soothe me.

_____

_____

_____

_____

_____

_____

_____

_____

_____

_____

_____

_____

_____

_____

This is some of what you are grieving. Perhaps this is the time for a good cry. When ready, move on to the next exercise.

How These Losses Affected You

Each of the losses you described has natural consequences. In the space that follows, write about how these losses (and any others that come to mind) impacted you. For example, without these losses you may have become more socially confidant, less depressed, or picked better partners. You can also reflect on what would have better supported your development. For example:

- There would not have been more children than Mother could handle, and she would have had more time for me.
- We'd have had more financial resources, and she could have been home more.
- I would have had the chance to start my [sport, interest, art] earlier, which would have led to more opportunities.

Write in whatever form you wish about how the losses of your childhood impacted you.

_____
_____
_____
_____
_____
_____
_____
_____
_____

Of course, there are no guarantees that you would have achieved or experienced all of these more positive things (mothering is only one factor among many), but seeing the losses may help you hold yourself with more compassion.

It is when you have mourned your losses and moved through your natural grief process that you reach the deepest healing. You may feel as if you can't survive the grief, but you can. Not only will you feel a lot lighter and have more energy on the other side of this grief, but the grief will also have tenderized you in ways that make you a more sensitive and compassionate person. Rather than your heart merely breaking, it can break open.

Why Does Healing Take So Long?

Working through pain is slow because we all have built-in defences and resistance to feeling pain. With the right support and practice, we can learn to tolerate uncomfortable feelings. This allows us to drop our defences and let our experience flow more unimpeded.

The work is also slow for another reason: You're rebuilding your foundation. Having to compensate for what was there and shouldn't have been, or what wasn't there but should have been, left you with a foundation that is not as strong, resilient, or steady as it needed to be to support a vibrant life. So there is a lot of building to do. Chapters 11, 12, and 13 will help with that, but first let's circle back to your current relationship with Mother.

10

Exploring Your Current Relationship with Mother

It is sometimes hard to distinguish the you and Mum of the present from the you and Mum of your childhood. They are two relationships that overlap. It is not until you've worked through the formative and more powerful childhood relationship with Mum that you have the possibility of a more healed relationship with her as an adult, because that first relationship gets in the way. Going through the steps of healing (seeing clearly what was, understanding it more objectively, and working through the feelings) is what releases you from the grip of this past relationship.

This chapter will help you clean up some of the unresolved issues from your childhood relationship with Mum, update what has happened between you in the intervening years, better understand Mother, and assess what kind of relationship can work between you now. There is also a section for those who are no longer in physical contact with their mother.

Letting Go of Trying to Get from Mother What She Cannot Give

Over the years I've seen a lot of suffering in those who cling to the hope that an important person in their life will change and finally provide what they have been waiting for.

To recognize that a person is not going to change brings grief because you know that you'll never get what you long for. But you'll save yourself a lot of needless suffering if you work to come to terms with what Mother can and cannot do and stop expecting her to be anything other than she is. There can be relief in that—a release from your futile attempts to change what cannot be changed. Then you can go elsewhere to fill your cup.

"I Release You"

To get out of the trap of clinging to Mother, you first have to learn to let go of wanting from her what you wanted as a child. If you sense that you are still wanting Mum to meet you in a particular way, I recommend working through these steps. They'll need to be done in sequence, and you probably won't be able to do all of them in a single sitting, so set aside some time for each.

First, write a letter to Mum (which you will *not* send) telling her the ways she disappointed you. Share with her the ways you tried to get her attention and help, which was not forthcoming, and what it cost you. These costs may include damage to your confidence, sense of agency (ability to get what you want), sense of being worthy and lovable, or belief that your needs are not shameful or unreasonable and can be met.

Next, select a trusted person to listen as you read your letter out loud as if to your mother. A therapist, close friend, mentor, or support group are all good options. If you don't have one of these available, just read it out loud to yourself. Feelings are allowed here; you don't need to suppress your anger or hold back your tears.

If, and only if, you feel ready, continue to the releasing stage. Otherwise, give it some space. You can come back to it at another time. You can't rush the letting go. It happens when it is ready to happen. Using words and actions to symbolize letting go helps jump-start the process, but this isn't the end of it. This letting go will likely continue silently inside for some time. New interactions that stir up old dust, like your mother doing what you most hate, may slow it down, but any genuine letting go will not be undone. I offer the following suggestions as a model. Change them as you wish.

Imagine saying to Mother, "I release you from my expectations. You don't need to meet my needs now, and we cannot change our past. We each carry that in our own way. I am moving on to get what I need elsewhere."

Find a way to symbolize moving on. It might be ripping up or burning something, or removing or letting go of an object that represents your relationship with Mother.

Another way to approach this is to imagine an energetic cord tying your bodies together. Visualize cutting that cord. One healing practitioner recommends pulling out the roots so you don't leave anything behind. I've had sensitive people recoil just at the idea of doing this. I would guess this is twofold: shuddering at the thought of being so intimately connected with Mother and at all the reasons you are wrong to "kick Mother out." You might need to do some prep work before you're ready for this. One possibility is using a repeating question (page 121) such as, "What's right about letting Mother stay corded with you?"

"I Release Me from the Roles I Took On"

In this exercise we will explore how you accommodated Mother's shortcomings and we'll give you an opportunity to quit the "contract" you unconsciously made.

When raised by a mother who feels less than fully capable, you make adaptations you should not have to make. We looked at some of these in chapter 8 (pages 108 and 110). You may have taken on caretaking duties or become precociously independent, for example. It may take some unearthing to see what your adaptations were.

There are costs to these adaptations, and you may have some animosity about that. For example, a son treated as Mother's "Little Man" and assigned husband-like duties, like being her companion, may feel quite a bit of resentment. The worst is being saddled with Mother's dependence, feeling her needing you too much.

First, identify and describe as many of your adaptations as you can. What did you prohibit yourself from doing, and what did you feel compelled to do for the sake of protecting Mother?

_____
_____
_____
_____
_____
_____
_____
_____
_____
_____
_____
_____

Next, imagine Mother in front of you (give her a throne to sit on) and tell her what you will no longer do and not do for her sake. You are claiming the right to no longer make costly sacrifices to accommodate her. Write these out in the space that follows or invite in a trusted person to witness as you lay out these new rules of engagement.

_____
_____
_____
_____
_____
_____
_____
_____
_____
_____

Finally, send Mother on her way or close the conversation by saying something like, "I know this is a lot to hear, but it is important for our relationship, and I hope you can take it in."

Afterward, give yourself time to let your system metabolize this deep experience. Going for a walk, doing some stretching, or taking a nap are some of the best ways to give your system time to absorb a big change.

Understanding Mother

In moving into a new relationship with Mother, you need to add to your understanding of her using a wider view than you had as a child. A child doesn't have many data points and is more encompassed in a subjective reality than an adult who has more experience and points of comparison. What we understand shapes our interpretations of Mother's behaviours and our emotional responses to them. In the next exercise we invite in a first-person experience of Mother's life.

Writing Mother's Story

While it would be enlightening to have your mother tell her story in her own words, that's not always possible. In this exercise you are invited to tell her story *as if* she were telling it herself, although from a more transparent and self-aware place than she might be able to. You are trying to feel yourself into her life. Stretch as far as you can using empathy and conjecture. If you are too uncomfortable with conjecture, then simply note how little you know about her life. Why is that, do you think?

Write a one- or two-page narrative of your mother's life. Include in it a few sentences about each of the following.

- Her parents
- Her family situation as a child, including what the familial relationships were like, and what roles she seemed to play in the family
- Her late adolescence and what dreams she had for her life
- The circumstances of her pregnancy with you and how she felt when you were born
- Her experience as a mother

_____

_____

_____

_____

_____

_____

_____

_____

_____

_____

Exploring Your Current Relationship with Mother

How was that? Did anything surprise you?

Stepping Stones in Your Adult Relationship with Mum

In the years since you left your childhood home, many things have happened. You may have had children of your own, had important romantic relationships, and gone through the deaths of family members or other crises with your mother. You may have held a series of jobs that further shaped you. Maybe you've done therapy. A list of stepping stones is a good way to see which of these events has had the most impact on your relationship with Mother. (See page 41 if you want a refresher on stepping-stone lists.)

This list will cover from the time you left home to the present day. Make the list as long as you want and then, if necessary, cut it back to just eight to twelve items by marking those that feel most important. Write in abbreviated form, just as much as you need to identify each event.

Once you have made your list, read it through and reflect on it. What captures your attention? Were there major turning points? Did these bring you closer together, further apart, reverse roles in any way? What, if anything, do you most regret? Most appreciate? Write your reflections here.

What I Notice about Mother Now

Having learned what you have about Mother and your relationship, now let's reflect on your mother as a mother.

Using the following sentence starters, complete each sentence as feels right to you.

Watching Mother as an adult, something I notice is _____

_____

Compared to the best mothers I have seen, my mother _____

_____

I'd say my mother's best asset is _____

_____

Her greatest liability is _____

_____

Under stress, my mother _____

_____

My mother seems to view the mother role as _____

_____

If she could do it over again, I think my mother would _____

_____

I think she wishes that _____

_____

My mother has no clue that _____

_____

From more distance, I now see _____

_____

Take a moment to read through your responses, and then summarize what you learned.

_____
_____
_____
_____
_____
_____
_____
_____
_____

What Kind of Relationship with Mum Is Right for You?

It's natural not to know exactly what kind of relationship you want to have with Mother moving forward, if any at all. The next three exercises are designed to help flesh out important points to consider. Let's start by looking at what you what you like and enjoy about Mum. Why is it you might want a relationship with her?

What You Enjoy About Mum

We have been drawing back the curtain on things that are difficult in your relationship with Mother, but there may be some things about her that you appreciate and like to be around. Make a list of those qualities. They might be anything from a sense of humor to a skill that she has.

_____

_____

_____

_____

_____

_____

_____

_____

_____

After making your list, take a moment to reflect on how significant these qualities are to you. Maybe you value them enough that they outweigh some of the negatives, and maybe not. Are these more superficial things, such as her telling funny jokes, or are they ever helpful to you? Do you have others who provide these desired qualities?

If you could not think of any things you enjoy about Mum, this tells you something. It may be that you are too wounded by her to recognize any of her positive traits, or maybe those qualities only show up in rare moments and you can't bank on that.

Assessing Mother's Capacity for Relationship

Before settling on what kind of relationship you want to aim for, it's important to make an educated guess about what Mother is capable of now.

Rate Mum on a scale of 1 to 5 (5 being the highest) on each of the following.

	SCALE
Ability to take in information that is challenging	
Ability to not "think with her feelings" but see beyond her feelings	
Interest in knowing your experience	
Interest in knowing anyone's experience	
Orientation toward growth (doing hard work for the sake of becoming more mature)	
Ability to look with appreciative eyes; seeing others for who they are	
Ability to step out of a self-absorbed stance where "It's all about me"	
Capacity to be vulnerable, to show honest emotions	
Ability to articulate her experience	
Capacity for closeness	
Ability to show affection and warm feelings	

	SCALE
Ability to be there for another	
Flexibility	
Ability to admit mistakes	
Ability to view situations with nuance	
Bandwidth to deal with something challenging	
Ability to talk about misunderstandings and hurts in relationships	
Ability to not get caught in her first reactive emotions	
Ability to approach things from compassion rather than judgment and blame	
Interest in investing in this relationship	

After rating Mother, add up all the points to determine roughly how capable she might be of having a more constructive relationship moving forward. A score of 20 (meaning you gave Mother a 1 in every category) is the lowest possible, and 100 (a 5 in every category) is the highest.

A higher score means there is a better chance of being able to improve the relationship. The more vulnerable you feel, the higher the score you likely need in order to feel comfortable giving a relationship with Mum a chance. In addition to this attempt at quantifying her capacity, you can also use it to note particular strengths and weaknesses.

Based on all of this, how capable do you think Mother might be of having an improved relationship?

_____

We've tried to make an educated guess at what Mother is capable of, but it's not the end of the tale. Adult children are often shocked when Mother makes a huge positive transformation with no clues that this was coming and no understanding of what created this change. You want to be realistic about what seems possible so you're not holding on to hopes that are ungrounded, but not shut the door to the possibility of changes that may seem like nothing short of miracles.

Looking at Your Own Capacities

Now let's realistically assess what you are capable of when it comes to refashioning a relationship with Mum at this time.

Rate yourself on a scale of 1 to 5 (5 being the highest) on each of the following.

	RATING
Orientation toward growth (doing hard work for the sake of becoming more mature)	
Ability to see others for who they are	
Ability to step out of a self-absorbed stance in which "It's all about me"	
Capacity to be vulnerable, to show honest emotions	
Ability to articulate your experience	
Capacity for closeness	
Ability to admit mistakes	
Ability to talk about misunderstandings and hurts in relationships	
Ability to not stay trapped in reactive emotions	
Ability to approach things from compassion rather than judgment and blame	

Since there are half as many items here, the top score you can receive is 50. If you like working with 100 as the top score, just double your score. Note your score here, and also how you feel about it.

_____
_____
_____
_____
_____
_____

Now answer this question: How much energy do I have to put into working on this relationship right now?

Take into account situational factors (kids, work, partner issues), how important the relationship is to you, and where you are in your healing journey. Given everything you've learned, is working on this relationship what you want to be doing?

_____
_____
_____
_____
_____
_____

It's a lot of work to go from numbly following a prescribed role (exactly what Mother may have done!) to working out what kind of relationship fits for you at different stages of your life and healing. It will change. Any real relationship is something you need to keep up with.

There are also entangling factors that may affect what you feel free to do with this relationship. You may be invested in keeping a relationship with other family members who, for various reasons, think you must not leave Mum. Maybe you and Mum belong to the same community organizations and this makes it awkward. Sometimes there are assets, like an inheritance, you don't want to ruin all chances of receiving. The decision about the type of relationship you want is never simple.

It's important to recognize that there is not one right way for everyone to follow. Your job is to find what is right for you and to keep updating that. You may need to set boundaries with a mum who is intrusive and acts as if your job is to make her life run smoothly. You may need to have no contact for an unspecified amount of time. You might demote Mum from a central role to a minor character or push her off the stage altogether. Or you might go along with the familiar script for a while, buying time while you sort things out. No one can determine this for you. It may feel excruciating or impossible to act against your prescribed role, but sometimes you need to learn to do the impossible in order to free yourself.

Should You Forgive?

Some people will tell you to forgive Mum and not make her a problem anymore. This may work for some people some of the time, but it's a little more complicated than that. The problem is that you can have a moment that feels transformative, but it doesn't last. You feel forgiving, but then other moments follow in which you are not forgiving. That seems to be how it is with feelings, one following and contradicting another. One explanation is that parts of you forgive while others hold a grudge. The work with inner child parts in the next chapter helps make sense of this.

Forgiving doesn't erase all the impacts of someone's behaviour or negate their responsibility for what they've done. Forgiveness is more like saying, "I know you messed up. It cost me a lot. In my heart I still care about you. I won't throw you away because of it." I see forgiveness less as an act of will and more as the heart's spontaneous movement.

Often there is a primal bond we are not letting ourselves feel. It is blocked by anger and hurt lying on top of it. Many say that there is love underneath, but maybe the emotional distance is so great between you that there is nothing left, any natural caring snuffed out long ago. And maybe that is true at one point and no longer true at another due to intervening experiences. We can only walk this journey one step at a time.

There are several resources you can turn to for more help with this complex process. In her book *I Thought We'd Never Speak Again: The Road from Estrangement to Reconciliation*, Laura Davis reminds us that mending a broken relationship happens over time, involves inevitable setbacks, and doesn't follow a script. (It doesn't always involve talking things out, for example.)

Susan Forward provides a bit of a road map for those thinking of "divorcing" their mother in her book *Mothers Who Can't Love: A Healing Guide for Daughters*.

How You Feel About Forgiving Mum

This sentence-stem exercise is a good way to examine your feelings about forgiving Mum. Complete the following.

When someone says I should forgive Mum, I feel _____

_____

How can forgiving _____

_____?

One reason I don't forgive her is _____

_____

I can't forgive her until _____

_____

I would forgive her if _____

_____

I have moments of forgiving, and then _____

_____

In other relationships, what helps me forgive is _____

_____

Good work! There is no agenda here except to help you explore this subject.

Sharing Opinions on Forgiving Mum

People have quite different opinions on the need to forgive parents and how to do that. This exercise offers you a chance to talk it out with peers, with no one proclaiming one right way.

I generally suggest that when doing work with partners or groups, you avoid what is called "crosstalk" (responding to each other without permission). You can use that framework here, too, each taking a turn to talk about how you think about forgiveness without others chiming in, or you can have a more interactive conversation. The one thing that is not acceptable is any kind of judgment about how someone else approaches forgiveness. The value here is in having a safe space to catch up with where you are.

Wise Self-Protection

Your relationship with Mother has hurt you, and being a good mother to yourself now requires that you protect vulnerable parts of you. It doesn't mean you go around in heavy psychological armor but that you know what destabilizes you and think out ways to avoid that.

If Mother tends to lash out, you quickly stop her, verbally and nonverbally showing her that you are not going to stand for being attacked. If she drags you down with her neediness, you are aware of the pattern, discern what is true need and what is felt need, habit, or manipulation, and give yourself a choice about whether and how to respond. In other words, you have boundaries. This is one of the most glorious things about being an adult. You can, as good parents often tell their children, "Use your words" (although that is not the only element in setting boundaries). Not that this guarantees a respectful or reasonable response from Mother, but you can do it for you, and you can remove yourself from abusive situations.

With a mother who is more emotionally cut off, you are less likely to be attacked and more likely to be abandoned. The risk in pursuing a relationship is that Mother may disappear and leave you alone with your feelings, unheard once again. You can't stop Mother's abandoning behaviours, but if you can name these for yourself and tie them back to her lack of awareness or capacity, you may cushion yourself a little. Equally or more important is that you respond to the hurt this leaves you with, so you aren't also abandoning yourself.

It is important to feel safe in your current relationship with Mum, and thus it's important to do some prep work. You'll want to be aware of what feels painful so you can prearrange interactions, intervene in the moment, or later do some self-repair around the wounding that happens despite your best efforts. The following exercise will help you make a plan.

Protecting Yourself from Further Hurt or Abuse

Use the following questions to guide you in setting boundaries, addressing as many as you can in the space that follows.

- In what situations do you most easily feel hurt or mistreated in your current relationship with your mother?
- Where might more boundaries be helpful?
- What are some things you could do to establish and reinforce those boundaries?
- What will likely never change? How do you feel about that?
- What helps you recover after challenging times with Mum?

_____
_____
_____
_____
_____
_____
_____
_____
_____
_____

Getting Group Support

Not everyone in your group may have a current relationship with their mother, but they can still listen. This is a chance for those of you who feel a need to "up your game" in terms of decreasing attack or abandonment by Mum to share your thoughts and get support. Use this time to talk about strategies you haven't tried before or that you hope to make more effective. I suggest each group member take 4 or 5 minutes to share, and then allow brief feedback, centered around resources and encouragement. It's a slippery slope into giving advice, so decide as a group what the limits are beforehand.

Being Truer to Yourself

We often fail to give ourselves a chance to retreat into our cave to do our inner work. We don't feel free of cultural expectations, Mother's expectations, or our own self-imposed requirements. This forces us to act in a way that is not true to ourselves.

A common example is deciding what to do when you can't honestly celebrate your mother on Mother's Day. Do you send the least dishonest card you can find, not acknowledge her at all, or do what you think she would like, simply to avoid rocking the boat? Can you give yourself permission to be true to you, even if it leads to Mother feeling hurt? Or does this stress you out so much that it doesn't feel worth it?

Becoming truer to yourself is an important step toward a more healed life and more healed relationship with yourself. It is something that happens one step at a time.

One Small Step

In this exercise I want you to identify one change you could make to be more true to yourself when it comes to your current relationship with Mum. Perhaps it is saying no to a request or expressing a feeling you wouldn't ordinarily show. It might be going away for a holiday that you have typically spent with Mother in the past, such as traveling somewhere new without her. What is one small step toward your freedom?

When Mother Is No Longer Part of Your Life

Your mother may no longer be in your life for several reasons. She may be so severely compromised that she is not really "here," you may have cut off contact years ago, or she may have died. Even if this is the case, there is still value in working on this relationship and it's still is a way for you to communicate. Instead of speaking by phone or face-to-face, you can speak to her overriding consciousness or soul. Communicating this way has some advantages; in this state you'll find Mother more open, more self-aware, and more caring.

You can do this simply in your mind, but I'm encouraging you to use the dialogue method we've used before. If it's written, you can come back, reread, and reflect on it again, and it keeps your mind focused on the task. Remember, in a dialogue, you start a new line with each change in speaker.

Dialoguing with Mum

Take a moment to collect your thoughts about what you want from this exercise. When you are ready, start the conversation from as honest a place as possible and from your current self rather than a reactive part like a hurt or angry child. This means you report your feelings rather than hurl them at her. You might begin, "Mum, I have some things I want to say to you . . ." You could speak about how you experienced the relationship, how this impacted you, what you wanted from her, your disappointment or anger—anything that wants to be said.

Remember that as her spiritual self, Mother has more capacity. So, if what would have stopped you in real life is that she would have shut you down or turned away, imagine that she is able to listen now. Mother is not the only one who is being asked to listen. You need to be willing to listen, too.

Don't be too quick to conclude that the dialogue is not working. You may need to sit patiently while listening for her response and, at some point, continue on if you don't perceive anything. It may take several tries to establish the connection before you succeed. If it's been a while, you may need a little time to warm up to each other again. You also need to be in as clear and receptive a state as possible. Once they get going, conversations take on a life of their own, even with interruptions.

Go until the dialogue feels at a close for now. Thank Mother for participating. Then give yourself some time to absorb it all.

Congratulations on doing all this hard work on your relationship. Like everything else, the work will continue, and you now have more data to use as you go forward.

11

Parenting Your Young Parts

We come now to a third lens through which to view (and treat) the problems we discuss in this book. The first lens focuses on the incredible impact of parenting and our early years. In chapter 7 we added the lens of trauma. A benefit of adding that lens is its focus on the nervous system, which informs many trauma therapies. Trauma is believed to have set (or reset) the nervous system, making it harder to maintain calm.

Our third lens comes specifically from models that acknowledge different parts of the self. We are not one homogeneous thing. There are distinctive parts of us, often in conflict with each other. Each has its own needs, motivations, beliefs, memories, and flavor. Parts therapy, or parts work, describes parts as "like real people." Let's learn more about how to become familiar with them.

An Introduction to Parts Work

Understanding that there can be parts of the self that hold different histories and know different things from the whole was a rather radical discovery. Leading-edge therapists have worked with parts for over fifty years, although it is only in recent decades that it has become more mainstream.

One form of parts work, known as inner child work, was popularized in the 1990s, although I generally use the term *child parts* rather than *inner child* because there is no unitary inner child. These child parts need your help. Some are flailing, upset, feel abandoned and stuck. You are the one who can best parent them now.

The more trauma there has been in someone's life, the more frozen and exiled child parts there will be. It would be a mistake, however, to believe all child parts are wounded. I have found, for example, a natural child in me who is a source of great wisdom and a refreshing honesty that leaves everyone laughing.

Just as we talked about collapsing into emotions, we often collapse into or are "blended" with parts and not aware of them. For example, an outside observer sees you as behaving *like* a child in a tantrum, but you are so in the tantrum that you don't recognize the adult here that is acting as a child. Another example is getting stuck in a pattern of self-soothing without recognizing that it is a child part that needs soothing, which you could more deliberately provide from an adult state while still having two feet on the ground.

One strategy that may help when you're collapsing into a child part is to look at your body and notice it is the body of an adult. Another way to decipher what is actually going on is to begin a dialogue in your journal. This makes room for more voices to be recognized. Content that has a harder time breaking into your normal thinking has more room to show up in writing. If you hear something like "It's too awful! Nobody helps me! I can't do this by myself!" while writing, it is easier to recognize this as a part speaking up. Otherwise, you may not know why you feel stuck and unable to move forward.

Parts work progresses from whatever is the most accessible entry point (perhaps an older child part who knows a little more about the others) to deeper dimensions, which usually means to more edgy material and younger, more wounded parts. Remember that you can always uplevel your support by finding a therapist to help with this. There are numerous therapies that use parts work, some very simple and some much more complex. If in your work, you find voices (parts) that are scaring you, I recommend looking at Internal Family Systems (IFS) therapy, which is most versed in dealing with parts. It's better if you don't go in with the hope the therapist will become the parent these child parts yearn for. The therapist is there to help *you* become that good parent.

Parenting Your Child Parts

Parenting child parts requires skills similar to those needed to parent physical kids. These include empathy and attunement, prioritizing a child's needs, communication, and not getting so pulled away by the practical tasks of life that you lose the emotional connection. Just as with actual children, your emotional tone will be felt by these sensitive inner beings. You must come with sincerity, honesty, and as much love as you can muster. Child parts need to know you truly care about them.

You will likely meet various obstacles in the process of getting to know your inner children. These include the following.

- Feelings of inadequacy ("I don't know how to be with a child")
- Fears of getting in over your head and of having to feel the pain these parts carry
- Guilt for not having been there earlier
- Critical and dismissive parts that don't want you to take on this job
- Mistrust from child parts that may take time warming up to you

Just as you need to recognize when a child part is involved, that child has to recognize and accept you as someone who can help. Parts are very sensitive to how trustworthy you are. You must approach them with care and respect and not like an emotionally absent mother who may have been irritated or robotic.

Your relationship with child parts takes time to develop—time and consistency. You don't get to operate as a parent just when you want to, but rather need to be there through good times and bad. Emotionally absent mothers often miss both. Trust grows as parts feel safe, you keep your word, and you show that you are reliable. If you break your promises, you take two steps back.

Your task is to become the nurturing parent that a given child part needs. That may feel awkward at first as you may not have a good role model to follow. Although there are many qualities of a nurturing parent that are required in this project of re-parenting, the most important is the ability to show your love. Unfortunately, you might not yet have developed the ability to naturally express love as a nurturing parent would. If you've learned to show love anywhere (with partners, friends, pets), that helps. Animals are often the easiest and very forgiving. Even tending to plants can be a way of showing care for something. Your ability to show love will continue to grow as you practice and as you open your heart more.

If you are not sure you are ready to take on inner child work, the next two exercises may help you.

Exploring How You Feel About Taking on This Parenting Work

As you consider approaching this work (if it is new to you), it's good to check in with how you feel about it. Circle the words that best describe that.

nervous

hesitant

excited

unprepared

anxious

confidant

scared

inadequate

fearful

cautious but optimistic

out of my depth

wanting to help

Add any other words or phrases that describe how you feel.

_____

_____

_____

_____

_____

It's perfectly normal to have some ambivalence or to be nervous. You may recognize some of the reasons for this in the bulleted list on page 161. You may also have some judgments or a protector part saying, "Don't be ridiculous. This is stupid." Just as guilt keeps you from daring to criticize Mother, such reactions are trying to stop you from doing this work.

Communicating with Parts

There are many ways to connect with child parts. These include dialoguing in a journal, speaking inwardly (or out loud) with them, holding props (like a teddy bear or doll), or putting your arms around your own body while imagining holding your child. Once you've established trust, this can be comforting to both of you.

You want to make available a number of ways for these parts to communicate with you—especially the youngest ones. You can let them use art materials or the equivalent of play therapy, showing through actions what it is they want to express. You can even use a sandbox or a sand tray as some therapists use, with figurines that you let act out the feelings and dynamics between parts. Have some fun. Healing child parts is not only about holding old pain, but also nourishing that child with activities the child wants more of. Ask your parts for direction. How do they like to express themselves?

Sending an Invitation

Here is a concrete step to begin your work with inner child parts. If you are already doing this work, just skip this exercise.

In the space provided, write out what you would say as a first conversation with your inner child parts. Explain why you are doing this, and why now. Be as honest as possible, even sharing your nervousness. Put it out as an invitation. Let them know you want to get to know them and will be back soon. You can write it out and then speak it aloud, if that feels right to you.

I have separated this first conversation from the next exercise, but they could also be combined. Before you get started you might read the next exercise so if things are already rolling, you are prepared. If you want to stop after just this first exercise, that's fine as well.

_____

_____

_____

_____

Meeting a Child Part

After indicating your intentions, as in the previous exercise, here is a model you can continue with, based once more on dialoguing.

Go back and forth between the points of view of two or more parts, changing lines each time you switch. Use a letter or symbol to represent who is talking. Since dialogues can take considerable space, you may want to have extra paper on hand or use your journal rather than this workbook. As always, when doing intentional inner work, make sure you are not likely to get interrupted and your environment is conducive to the work, such as being free of distractions and feeling safe.

On your first line, write something like, "Hi. I'd like to get to know you." This is an opportunity for any child part that is willing to step up. Be curious but not demanding. You might consider asking how old it is, what name this child would like to be called, what emotions it carries. No one likes to be peppered with questions, so think of this more as a listening session. Go back and forth using your best listening skills, including empathy. Let the conversation go as long as it naturally does, then thank the part and say goodbye for now.

Pause for a moment to see if another part pops up, then do the same thing. Continue until you come to a stopping place.

_____

_____

_____

_____

_____

_____

_____

_____

If you had a part (or more than one part) come up during this exercise, kudos to you! You are on your way! Your path to strengthening these relationships will continue to open up. In fact, your parts will help you. With time and experience, you will evolve from a reluctant parent to a confident one.

Enjoying a Nourishing Activity Together

The goal of this exercise is to spend enjoyable time with a younger part of you. It is appropriate to ask what this child would like to do, but you can also do some guesswork and build on actual experience over time, repeating what works well.

Settle on an activity you think both of you would enjoy. Maybe it is sledding or going to a water slide, or baking cookies and watching a movie. It could be finger painting or some other creative activity or something simple like going to a special place to watch a sunset. It's good to have things you do together, just the two of you, but you can also invite others. Sometimes young parts like being with other people. They don't want to be hidden away, isolated.

Consider this a homework assignment; after completing it, return here and write how it went.

_____
_____
_____
_____
_____
_____
_____
_____
_____
_____
_____
_____
_____

Doesn't it give you hope to have this much fun parenting your adult self?

12

Self-Care as Mothering

In chapter 3 we talked about the many aspects that together constitute mothering. Self-care includes a great many of those and is essentially the way you mother yourself now.

Self-care goes way beyond our usual ideas about eating well and exercising. It includes a much wider range of activities and addresses how you do these things—whether with attunement, gentleness, and real care, or more impersonally, just doing what you think needs to be done. We're talking about feeding your body, taking care of your health, how you talk to yourself and attend to your hurts, and how encouraging or critical you are.

Self-Talk

Self-talk is the chatter inside your head. It generally sounds like someone else talking to you, but it's really a part of you that is doing the talking and is often an internalization of someone important in your life. This voice is frequently modeled on a critical parent, saying things that the parent might say or think. There can also be a positive and supporting voice, but most of us will need to develop that.

The critical voice has been given several names. The most common is Inner Critic, but it is also referred to as a Critical Parent. I'll simply call it your "critic." The critic says things like "You idiot!" or "Klutz!" or "You're talking about yourself too much. See how self-absorbed you are?"

It's not that you physically hear these words—you hear them as thoughts. They may form their messages using the word "you" as in the previous examples, or it may use the "I" format ("I'm so selfish"). Sometimes that chatter may be going on at a subvocal level, and you may only feel the impacts of it, such as feeling discouraged and beaten down. Becoming more aware of your stream of thoughts helps ferret out these voices, which you can then deliberately work to change.

Recognizing Your Critic

Let's practice identifying what your critic says to you. Consider areas where you tend to get down on yourself, such as your appearance, certain personality traits, and skills. What judgments do you recognize? Are these constructive things you would say to a good friend? Or are they a little too mean for that? Demeaning and overly critical messages come from your critic.

In the left-hand column, list some of the things you hear in your mind that are critical and leave you feeling bad. Then, in the right-hand column, write down where you've heard something like that before. These messages may have been said in very stark and even nasty ways, but these same messages could also have been relayed without words. For example, someone's impatient behaviour may communicate that you are too slow.

All of us are saddled with some of these thoughts, and we need to practice counterbalancing (or replacing) them with a supportive voice modeled on what you imagine a really good mother or great support person would say. An in-your-corner voice will lead to better behaviour than a "dressing down" will. Using the parenting frame, this voice is your Nurturing Parent.

Incorporating a generous kind of support in your self-talk is one way to parent your adult self. It won't come automatically, but you can develop it over time. You start by being intentional. Later, this supportive voice may show up more spontaneously.

Here are the kinds of messages you could incorporate into your self-talk.

- You did your best. I'm proud of you.
- You didn't mean to hurt anyone. You were just being yourself. I love you.
- I think you can do it.
- Yay! That was fabulous!
- You are strong, and I am behind you.

Trying Out New Messages

Now let's try on a Nurturing Parent voice, using messages that are meaningful to you. Select a couple of Nurturing Parent messages you would like to incorporate into your self-talk. Use short, easy-to-remember ones, like "I know you can do it" and "I'm proud of you." It could be a popular phrase like "You go, girl!" Write down three to five in the space that follows.

_____

_____

_____

_____

_____

Now that you have a few that feel good to you, your task is "install" them by deliberately using them. (You might put Post-it notes around as a reminder.) When a few favorites show up in your self-talk more regularly, you can use the same process with additional messages.

Often there will be a negative outburst from another part in response to positive self-talk just as there may be to the use of affirmations. If you encounter this, see if this part will dialogue with you. Does it believe it is dangerous for you to feel good about yourself? Why does it want to take any positive messages away from you? If this gets more involved than feels doable without more help, I'd recommend looking at books about the Inner Critic or parts work, such as Internal Family Systems, to get to the bottom of this.

It's hard to set and follow an intention on your own without some kind of accountability or support. It helps if you can share your intention and progress with a supportive person. (Maybe they'll want to join you by practicing with their own nurturing messages.) You can also work in an ongoing way in your journal, checking in, studying what gets in the way, practicing being supportive, and noting how that feels. Has it changed the critical voice at all?

Good Self-Care Now as the Attuned Mothering You Missed

Before you could take care of yourself, your care came from Mother. Emotionally absent mothers were "missing in action" to some degree, so their care was either spotty or, in too many cases, totally missing.

Sometimes care duties (the "what") are met, but in a way that is mis-attuned (the "how"). For example, you might remember being touched mechanically or coldly by Mother while being bathed, or being touched roughly while she brushed your hair or dressed you.

It's too easy to unconsciously continue that legacy in your own self-care. The first step to making change always begins with awareness—noticing what you are feeling or why you are doing something. I had a client who noticed feeling "I hate taking care of you" when putting lotion on her skin. She recognized this came from internalizing the sense that her mother hated taking care of her. You can imagine, then, that this woman took on this self-care duty more out of duress (like when her skin was so dry that it was literally cracking) than in a way that would have actually helped make up for the gentle, loving care she had missed.

Getting a Sense of Your Current Level of Self-Care

In the space that follows, write about how you tend to care for yourself, speaking to as many of the following areas as you can.

- Paying attention to how your body responds to foods or activities and adjusting your behaviours (for example, not eating what doesn't agree with you)
- Responding to your health and medical needs
- Giving yourself a choice about participating in activities rather than doing what you've always done or think you should do
- Allowing yourself comforts, including ample rest
- Paying attention to your emotional needs

Showing Yourself Love

Imagine for a moment that a Fairy Godmother taps you with her wand and awakens a Nurturing Parent inside of you. This Nurturing Parent sends you the following letter explaining how she will take care of you. Complete the sentences that haven't been filled in yet and then continue in the space that follows with more statements of your own.

To My Precious One,

I want so badly to show you how much you mean to me. Words can sometimes feel hollow, so I will show you through my actions as well as through words.

Rather than touch you in a cold or clinical way, I want you to experience my touch as saying "You are dear to me."

Rather than feed you whatever is convenient, I will _____

_____.

When you are sick, I will _____.

When you are worn out, I will prop up a pillow and make you comfy and tell you that you've done enough.

When you are pushing yourself too hard, I will _____

_____.

When you are unhappy, I will _____

_____.

When you are worried about something, I will _____

_____.

When you won't get off the couch, I will _____.

When you have to do something that requires great courage, I will _____

_____.

When you are doing things that are not good for you (from drug addictions to doomscrolling), I will _____

_____.

_____

_____

_____

_____

_____

_____

_____

With all of these things, I want you to remember that you are important and precious to me.

Love,
Your Nurturing Parent

What did it feel like to write from that loving voice? If you found yourself rolling your eyes, see that as a defence. You are dismissing what you see as unreachable. I'm here to tell you that if you take little steps, this Nurturing Parent can become real.

Taking Care of Your Body

Many of us have not learned to nourish our bodies. Too often, we learned to give them the minimum needed—and even then, somewhat grudgingly or haphazardly. We often relate to our bodies as our emotionally absent mother related to us. I'm not only referring to how Mother treated your body but how she treated all of you. It's just that now—without your knowing it—the body holds the burden you carried as a neglected child.

Our basic physical needs include good food (that agrees with and aids the operation of the body), sleep, water, movement, good touch, and what we call "creature comforts," which are material conditions that serve our sense of comfort and safety, such as a nice place to stay, or being warmed by a fire or the arms of someone you love.

Appropriate health care is also part of this list. That starts with noticing when your body needs some help—whether that's your teeth or your toes, your digestion, your eyes, your joints, and so on. It's a matter of both noticing what is ailing *and* what you do in response, which comes in part from your attitudes. So let's take a look at these.

Responding to Your Body's Health Needs

With this exercise, we'll identify how you respond to your body's needs (including health care) and compare this with your mother's care of you.

Put your initials in front of each action that is true for you, and an M next to each that describes how your mother cared for you as a child. Some actions may have only your initials, some only an M, for "mother," some both, and some neither.

_____ Ignore physical symptoms as long as possible

_____ Do what is needed, but with resentment

_____ Seem to blame my body for not maintaining perfect health

_____ Overshoot health issues with an all-or-nothing kind of thinking, often going for a "fix" that involves more medical intervention than may be needed

_____ Not checking in with all parts of you about what kind of intervention is a good match

_____ Responding only to undeniable needs, overlooking optional care and what could be done to improve health. This may correspond to being unwilling to spend money or not wanting to put much effort into my care.

_____ Responding only when convenient, often overriding your body's daily needs (to hydrate, move, rest, and so on)

How would you rate yourself on a scale of 1 to 5 (5 being the highest) on responding to your body's needs? To what extent are you merely copying Mother? What would you like to do differently, if anything?

How You Feed Your Body

There are many factors that go into your habits around food and eating. You may have learned good and/or bad habits in your childhood home. In this exercise we'll take a look at your current habits and consider how well they are serving you.

To what extent are your meals rushed, or eaten while your attention is elsewhere? (This is the norm for many people, but it isn't good for digestion.) How often do you have a leisurely meal in a relaxed setting?

_____

_____

_____

_____

_____

How deliberate are your food choices? Are they convenience-based, or do you also take into account what your body wants (you can ask it!) and what is actually nutritious, free of harmful ingredients, and known to agree with you? Often, we continue eating foods that harm our health without connecting the dots between what we are eating and how we feel afterward.

_____

_____

_____

_____

_____

Do you notice when you've had enough, or do you tend not to stop until the food is gone or you can't eat another bite?

Do you fall into "emotional eating" where you eat simply to soothe yourself?

Do you take time to prepare healthy meals? Do you have healthy food for snacks?

How do your ways of eating compare to what you grew up with?

_____

_____

_____

_____

_____

_____

_____

_____

Now identify what you'd like to change, and plan some supportive structure for making these changes. For example, you can intentionally fill your plate with a more modest serving and then go back for more if you really want it, turn off your devices, or limit the availability of foods that are less healthy or that you overindulge in. How you feed yourself is an important indicator of the level of your self-care.

Write down a few ways you can support yourself in forming healthier eating habits.

_____

_____

_____

_____

_____

_____

_____

_____

Taking In the Care

Your efforts to take care of yourself can help make up for what you missed earlier—but only if you register it. If your system doesn't recognize that it is being given what it needs, your conscious or unconscious will still be branded by the old sense of being deprived and always wanting more.

If, on the other hand, you can register the good coming in from your self-care, it will change you, and your desperation (clinging) or rejection (closedness) won't be as likely to keep others at bay. Then you can receive from the inside (you) and the outside (others). Sounds good, doesn't it? This topic of getting enough nourishment is so important that I'm devoting the next chapter to it.

13

Taking In Nourishment

Mother is the designated first source of nourishment and nurturance. When mothered properly, you are not only provided what you need to grow but also taught to seek out and take in that which helps you thrive. If the first years of your life did not provide that nourishment, you may instead learn to do without.

I don't want that for you—a lifetime of "doing without," of not getting enough. I want you to orient to things that are nourishing and get plenty of them. These can help fill the holes left by a mother who wasn't fully there.

How You Experience the World

We each have a filter that shapes how we perceive and experience the world. In chapter 7 we talked about schemas and their function as filters. Just as the lens in a pair of eyeglasses can help sharpen your vision or cloud it, your overall schema of the world affects how warm or how mistrusting you feel toward others.

To help you discover what your lens is, make a check mark next to the following statements that best describe how you tend to think of the mass of people you don't know ("the world").

____ You have to watch out, as people often take advantage of you.

____ There is a lot of love in the human heart, and people like to help.

_____ When I ask for help, I can count on getting it more often than not.

_____ People don't really care about each other—or at least, people don't care about me.

_____ No one has time for other people. It's easier to just take care of myself.

_____ People don't give without wanting something back. You'd better know the price before you accept help.

In object relations theory, a branch of psychology, there's an idea that the fundamental way we experience the world grows out of our earliest relationship with Mother. If Mother is experienced as cold and uncaring when we are a helpless infant, we may develop a template where the world is ungiving and doesn't care about us. If Mother shows that she will be there and generously meets our needs, it is easier for us to trust both life and other people.

There are two things you should know: The first is that your image of the world is subjective and is highly colored by your early experience. Second, and even more important, is that you can change your filter. It will take time. Along the way, you need to challenge the old filter, noting, for example, when you are coming from mistrust when you don't need to. Healing comes as you open to new formative experiences.

You cannot change the world you grew up in, but you can change the world you live in now by working to be receptive to the good. Your world doesn't need to mirror your experience of your first years of life. What you want is to be open to the good things that life can offer.

Softening

You don't just flip a switch and go from your adaptation of making do with less to going after and enjoying an abundant life. It's a learning process, and you will need to lean into it.

In order to support yourself when your life was lacking basic support and to protect yourself from what seemed harsh or uncaring, you hardened (physically and emotionally). Hardening can show up in momentary ways like in a rigid posture or stern, closed-off facial expression, but that which is habitual becomes carried in our structure, and that posture often resculpts our body. This hardened appearance works to keep people away, which is often the unconscious motive. We harden to keep safe.

Just like hardened earth doesn't easily absorb water, this hardening gets in the way of absorbing the nourishment that can help you heal. To go from being impervious to nourishment to allowing it in, you need to learn to soften. That involves many pieces and will happen over time, but one of the things that helps is to consciously soften your body. Notice where there is tension and let go to the degree you can. This may lead to feeling more vulnerable, but that is something you'll get used to and which will diminish over time.

It also aids this softening when you expose yourself to things that are inspiring, when you practice sitting with vulnerable feelings when they first begin to emerge, and when you learn to be soft and kind to yourself.

Taking In Kindness

It's nourishing to feel you live in a world where there is kindness and you matter. One of the legacies of being under-mothered is not having a clear sense of that. Years ago, my therapist commented to me, "It's as if you need an ongoing drip of kindness." That "drip of kindness" may come in large ways (for example, a partner who is able to show their love) or in small, everyday ways—even with strangers. Do you notice when a clerk wants to be helpful? Can you take in something as simple as a smile or an attempt to connect? Can you take in even the smallest act of generosity? Take a moment to look for the kindness that has graced your life.

Identifying Kindness That Has Nourished You

Sit quietly and let come to mind moments when others have been kind to you. These may include small gestures you didn't much notice at the time or life-changing moments. Make a list of these, using just enough description for you to identify the incident.

_____

_____

_____

_____

_____

_____

_____

_____

_____

_____

Read through your list, close your eyes, and feel what it was like for you to receive someone's generosity. This marinating in past acts of kindness helps us recognize future kindness more easily.

It's not always easy to take in kindness. If you have a chip on your shoulder, it gets in the way. If you think you have to fight for every crumb you get, it gets in the way. If you don't know how to receive, it gets in the way. That's why we do this healing work.

Taking In Nurturing Touch

In chapter 6 we looked at your history of touch and where it has left you. Here, we turn to it again, this time to help make up for what was missing.

Sources of Good Touch

Let's take a look at where you currently get good touch and how you can get more of it. *Good touch* is noninvasive, sensitive to the receiver, and gives the receiver ways to modify it.

Make a list of situations (such as close relationships, massage, dance, sports) in which you've received good touch in the last half year. Cross out any that are no longer available.

_____
_____
_____
_____
_____
_____
_____
_____
_____
_____
_____
_____
_____
_____

Now think about how and where you may add to your "good touch supply." You might keep this list handy and cross out any that don't work out and add others that do.

Learning Your Touch Language

To learn what kind of touch nourishes you, it can help to experiment with your own touch. I have set this out as an exercise, but the real goal is for it to become more of an ongoing practice. The more aware you are of how your body prefers to be touched, the more you can bring this to your interactions.

Try the following experiments.

- Touch your body in a way that says, "You are precious."
- Cradle your face with a loving hand.
- Spend some time exploring how different parts of your body like to be touched.

Now take some time to reflect on these experiments and answer the following questions.

- What was it like to touch yourself lovingly? Name other gestures that are loving.
- Where and what kind of touch feels most supportive? How might you use touch to express support to others?
- What kind of touch feels protective to you?

_____

_____

_____

_____

_____

_____

_____

_____

_____

The more you know about what feels good to you and what does not, the more you can share that with others from whom you want to receive nourishing touch.

A Healing Presence

I use the term *healing presence* to describe people who feel good to be around. They calm you, bring a sense that you are not alone, and help you feel safe and comforted. How can this not be nourishing?

Who can be a healing presence? It may be a family member (although in some families there may be no one who meets the criteria), a partner, a close friend and confidant, a mentor. I found that people who were under-mothered do better when they find people who can stand in for Mother at times, either as a child (such as a teacher or a friend's mother) or as an adult (perhaps a mother-in-law). You might have a psychotherapist who is a real touchstone and place of safety for you. We are generally talking about someone who is or was in your life for a while, but even in a one-time interaction, you can experience someone as a healing presence. This includes you, too; you can become a healing presence for yourself.

Although we are most often talking about another person, you may experience a pet, places in nature, and aspects of the spiritual realm as healing presences.

Who Has Been a Healing Presence for You?

Let's identify who is or has been a healing presence for you and where you may be overlooking possibilities.

First, make a list of those who have been a healing presence in your life.

_____
_____
_____
_____
_____
_____
_____

Note what qualities these different presences have in common. These point out what you especially need. Do you need someone who is quiet by nature and helps calm your nervous system? Someone affectionate? One who says supportive things and champions you? Someone who makes you laugh and pulls you out of a bad mood when you feel sour and contracted? List the qualities you need most in the space that follows.

_____
_____
_____
_____
_____
_____
_____

How might you add to your stable of healing presences? Write down a few thoughts. This might involve forming new relationships or taking better advantage of existing relationships. If you can, think of one actionable step to take; for example, contacting someone you haven't kept up with who always makes you feel good.

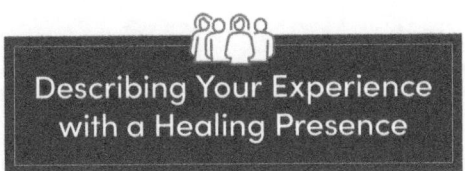

Describing Your Experience with a Healing Presence

This exercise can be done in a small group or with a partner. Make time for each of you to talk about a healing presence in your lives. Focus how this healing presence made you feel and how it impacted your life. When you are listening, do your best to serve as a healing presence for the speaker.

If you agree to feedback, keep it brief, like "I'm so glad you had that. It sounds like you felt [really loved by, safe with, protected, seen . . .]." This mirroring helps the sharer feel "felt."

It may be that you really can't identify any healing presence. If this is the case, the group can reflect something about that. ("That must be so painful. I can't imagine how alone you have felt.") Remember that words are less important than the nonverbal aspects communicated through voice and body language. If you want to provide touch, it's generally best to get permission first, although there are times when words fall short and what is most natural is to put a hand on someone's shoulder or touch their arm.

Nourished by Nature

Nature has been a refuge and safe place for many coming from violent, chaotic, or emotionally cold homes. Some experience it as a living, caring force. One woman relayed that the first time she heard the words "I love you," it was from a tree she was walking by as a young girl.

You don't have to be a rugged outdoor enthusiast or a dedicated tree hugger to enjoy nature. Being nourished by nature may be as simple as taking a walk along a beach or through a park, tending a garden, even just sitting outside. Being in nature helps you unwind, settle, and relax. I know many people for whom spending quality time in nature is a primary way they maintain their balance.

Where in Nature Do You Feel Most Held?

Let's identify the most powerful aspects of nature for you by using a few queries.

Let a memory come up of a time you felt connected to nature or at peace somewhere outdoors. What do you think contributed to that moment? What internal and external factors helped you be more present?

_____

_____

_____

_____

_____

_____

List some of your favorite places in nature, then see if you can identify the elements that make them so. For example, notice what types of terrain or bodies of water feel good to you.

_____

_____

_____

_____

_____

_____

_____

Now that you've identified this potent resource, you can turn to it more easily in times of need or for maintenance of your well-being.

Spiritual Sustenance

Spiritual feelings and experiences are not limited to such practices as meditation, prayer, and religious rituals; they are often connected to nature, beauty, and loving relationships. They also include "peak experiences," which are moments when you are overcome with awe, gratitude, or a sense of the perfection of things, even in the midst of everyday life.

Spiritual experiences are states of expansion: your consciousness expands, your feelings of connection and love expand, your ways of knowing expand. This is a great antidote to all the factors that limit us, including our conditioning and the limiting filters we talked about at the beginning of the chapter. It is in expansion that many find what is experienced as their true self.

Spirituality in more embodied forms is recognized everywhere and certainly throughout the physical world. There is also a vast invisible realm, in which you might experience non-physical presences like nature spirits, angels and guides, deceased ancestors, and revered religious figures such as various forms of the Divine Mother, the Christ, and the Buddha. Many report that the love, holding, protection, and guidance they experience from non-material sources far exceeds what any individual can provide.

Identifying Your Forms of Spiritual Nourishment

Where do you find spiritual nourishment? Is it looking up at a starry night sky? The sense of community you feel when singing in a choir or participating in an age-old religious ritual? Maybe it is working in your journal and uncovering an innocent part of your soul. Your list will be unique, as you are.

_____
_____
_____
_____
_____
_____
_____
_____
_____
_____
_____
_____

These resources are too important—too healing—not to make use of them, so I encourage you to make a point of regularly turning to them, particularly when you feel alone and unsupported.

Basking in Your Own Warmth

Don't forget that you are a source of nourishment for yourself. You can nourish yourself through small acts described in books on self-compassion and self-love. Sarah Peyton, author of *Your Resonant Self,* defines emotional warmth as when you feel held in a way that is just right for you. Doesn't that sound marvelous? That holding can happen in various ways, such as nurturing activities, guided meditations, supportive self-talk, and physical touch. When you extend warmth toward yourself, that is self-warmth.

Self-warmth can combat what others have called *self-coldness*. As a reader of this book, you understand the connections between how you treat yourself and how you've been treated. It's equally important to understand that you can change that legacy rather than maintain a coldness toward yourself reminiscent of how your mother was cold. Practicing self-warmth is one way to do this.

Taking in nourishment is not trivial. Taking in nourishment contributes to your healing every bit as much as all those tears you shed.

14

Bringing the Healing Forward

Your healing process will continue. It's great for you to continue to attend to it, which keeps it chugging along nicely, but for those who have committed to long-term healing it will continue beneath consciousness, inviting life to bring up situations that fuel it. I think the only situation in which it doesn't continue is for those who never began the journey, who have avoided it.

When in the thick of it, you may have little attention to spare for others, but even then your commitment to your own work can be an inspiration to others. As you come into more of yourself, the work you've done benefits all you come in contact with. It helps you become a better parent if you have children, a better friend, a better mate. There are an infinite number of ways you can contribute to the world, bringing the healing forward.

Being a Better Parent

If you have young children, probably the main challenge for you is stepping out of the legacy of your past and not repeating the patterns you learned. Staying consciously aware of these patterns and putting in the effort needed to do things differently are essential if you are not to automatically repeat what you lived and breathed every day of your young life.

It Stops with Me

You may have heard the statement, "It stops with me." Usually this refers to having gone through something that you swear not to carry forward to the next generation. In this exercise you'll identify what you do *not* want to pass on to your children—or *any* children.

Here are a few examples.

- I don't want any of my kids to feel like a "motherless child" as I did.
- I don't want my kids to have to look outside our family for a place to feel safe and cared for.
- I don't want to continue the pattern of never saying, "I'm sorry."

There is an opportunity in the next exercise to identify what kind of parent you want to be, so let this one focus on what you want to leave behind. Make a list of what you want to make sure *not* to carry forward.

_____
_____
_____
_____
_____
_____
_____
_____

Now read your list and let it become like a seed planted firmly inside of you. See your child (or children) thriving because you as a parent have vowed, "Let it stop with me."

Identifying What Kind of Parent You Want to Be

Use this sentence-stem exercise to define what you want to aim for as a parent. Answer it at least ten times, and feel free to use extra paper to continue if you like.

I want to be a parent who _____

_____,

I want to be a parent who _____

_____,

I want to be a parent who _____

_____,

I want to be a parent who _____

_____,

I want to be a parent who _____

_____,

I want to be a parent who _____

_____,

I want to be a parent who _____

_____,

I want to be a parent who _____

_____,

I want to be a parent who _____
_____,

I want to be a parent who _____
_____,

As you did in the last exercise, reread your list and envision it. You might enroll someone, ideally your parenting partner, in your intentions. Talk together about how your partner can support you, including how you want them to point out times you are slipping. If you don't have a partner, a friend (perhaps another parent) can be your ally in this way.

Naming Your Intentions

With a group or a single exercise partner, talk about what you want to do differently as a parent. For example, "I'm going to make sure that my kids know that I love them." Or "I aim to address any rupture that I am aware of within twenty-four hours." I suggest giving each person 4 or 5 minutes to speak without interruption. At the end of each person's sharing, provide a little support that is genuine, for example saying something like, "I can really see you doing that" or "These are great intentions and I'd like to support you along the way."

Giving What You Did Not Receive

It is normal for your earlier wounds to show themselves when anyone—including your own children—receive what you did *not* benefit from when growing up. Sometimes you may be happy for them, and sometimes that little "ouch" gets in the way. The more active the wound, the more likely it is to get in the way. (Think of it as a land mine that has not been deactivated.)

Something that may be triggering is when your child receives what you always wanted and never had—for example, when a teacher or neighbor lavishly praises your child. Generally, it's the child inside you that feels that "ouch." Note that and later take time to empathize with and comfort that child.

In this exercise, we'll look at the wounds that may come up and what you can do about them. First, make a list of things that you notice make you wince when you see them given to your child.

_____

_____

_____

_____

_____

_____

_____

_____

_____

_____

Now select one of the items from your list and write about why it's hard. You may not yet know why, but writing about it is one way to find out.

_____
_____
_____
_____
_____
_____
_____
_____
_____
_____
_____
_____
_____
_____
_____
_____
_____
_____
_____

Finally, consider what might help you not only be happy when your child receives this from someone else but also for you to be able to graciously provide it. It likely will involve working with your deprived child parts and perhaps making efforts now to provide what you missed and still long for. Another possibility is imagining your actual child standing in for you, and that your inner child is receiving what the outer child is receiving. Write down what you think will be most helpful to you.

_____
_____
_____
_____
_____
_____
_____
_____
_____
_____
_____
_____
_____
_____

Repeat steps 2 and 3 as many times as necessary, over multiple sessions if needed, to address other items on your list.

Hooray for you! You are changing the legacy.

Mothering the World

We don't only parent our children and ourselves. When we embody the qualities of a good mother, we bring them into the larger world. Remember, mothering is not just something you do for your biological children, and not something only women do. Our leaders need the qualities of good mothers. Earth needs caring stewardship. Humans and animals all need it.

The more you heal, the more warmth and wisdom you have to share. You can give and receive love more abundantly. In fact, you'll represent abundance rather than scarcity. Rather than feeling small, you'll feel big. Big enough to wrap others in your loving arms.

Identifying Healing Qualities You Can Offer

Let's look at what you currently offer and what you aspire to offer the world. These are all positive aspects of mothering. On each of the following lines, put an X where you see yourself now, and a star where you (realistically) aspire to be.

Showing empathy

———————————————————————

Protecting those who need it

———————————————————————

Providing holding and containment when needed

———————————————————————

Being affectionate (when appropriate)

———————————————————————

Encouraging and supporting others

———————————————————————

Being available for connection

———————————————————————

Being sensitive and responsive to the needs of others

———————————————————————

Guiding and shepherding others

Being willing to sacrifice when needed

Coming from "We" rather than "Me" (collaborating)

Everyone can cultivate these qualities. You may need to lean into it, but these are attainable goals. To make this more concrete, review your list and then write about what you most want to be able to embody and offer. Where is your growth edge, and what do you aspire to? For each goal, include what can support you in getting there.

_____

_____

_____

_____

_____

_____

_____

_____

_____

_____

_____

_____

_____

_____

Moments That Mirrored the Best of You

This exercise will make use of memories and emotions to help you identify what you have to offer.

Make a list of moments when you felt most yourself, highlighting something you feel good about. It may be when your heart was showing, when your wisdom was appreciated, when your unique ability to connect came into play, or when you were living your passion, your trust, or your faith. It may be when you felt the inherent goodness of you. Take a moment and see what memories come up. Meaningful moments like this might bring a tear to your eye or a feeling of recognizing something deeply true.

_____

_____

_____

_____

_____

_____

_____

_____

_____

_____

_____

_____

Now read through these and see how many you can hold at the same time. That's the *you* who can be a source of healing in the world, the you this world needs.

15

Reflecting on Your Journey

As we come to the end of this workbook, it's a good time to reflect on how far you've come. You've been on quite a journey, and it has changed you.

How Has This Journey Changed You?

Which of these statements do you most identify with?

____ I feel like I'm at the beginning of the journey, just now recognizing my pain.

____ I have a lot under my belt now but feel a long way from done.

____ I feel like I've come a long way and am really happy about that.

What feelings have changed since you started your work here? For example, you may not feel the same depth of grief when thinking about your childhood, or you may feel less gloomy. Some of your less desirable feelings may have lessened, and less familiar feelings that you enjoy may be showing up. Note them here. Take your time and look thoroughly.

_____

_____

_____

_____

_____

_____

What has changed in your relationships, both with Mother (if you have one with her) and with others? Think about how you respond to various triggers, how free you are to show your affection and vulnerability, what you might ask for and feel entitled to, your sensitivity to criticism and rejection, your clarity and ease in setting boundaries, and how transparent you can be.

_____

_____

_____

_____

_____

_____

_____

Name two triggers that have changed in some way. Maybe now, for example, when you see a loving mother-child interaction, you feel appreciation with only a tinge of sadness. Note: It's not all or nothing. Some triggers will disappear completely, and others may still be active. They point you to where there is still work to do.

_____

_____

_____

_____

_____

_____

_____

_____

What has changed in your identity and feeling about yourself? Do you feel less like an orphan in the world? Are there fewer wounded-child self-images? What qualities of your adult self do you see emerging?

_____

_____

_____

_____

_____

_____

_____

_____

_____

_____

Has your self-care changed in any way?

_____
_____
_____
_____
_____
_____
_____
_____

Are you putting more energy into what's nourishing for you, and do you feel any less absorbed by the pain of the past?

_____
_____
_____
_____
_____
_____
_____
_____

Have you sharpened or built new skills, like managing feelings, working in a journal, or empathizing with hurt parts?

_____
_____
_____
_____
_____
_____
_____
_____
_____

Which of these skills (or specific techniques) do you feel were the most helpful in your healing? Which do you want to carry forward with you?

_____
_____
_____
_____
_____
_____
_____
_____
_____

Name three things you want to continue to work on.

All this ground that you've covered shows just what a journey you've been on, and going on a journey is always to be honoured. It takes courage and strength.

Here is something that is important to remember: If you don't find yourself in a state of living happily ever after, you haven't failed. There will always be struggles and dark moments. Everyone has them!

Every step on your healing journey adds more support to your foundation, and the condition that you are healing is that of not having had an adequate foundation provided for you. You are the one creating that foundation, and you can strengthen it for the rest of your life.

We talked about healing in the first chapter, where I said that healing doesn't mean you never hurt again. Your healing shows up in how quickly you recover and in having more pain-free times. Healing allows for more room and more grace in your life, and this allows you to reach further. You've wrestled with your demons and emerged triumphant in the sense that you have learned to liberate yourself from their grasp. You don't need to stay small in order not to get pummeled. You have earned the right to take up space, go after what you want, and feel good about yourself. Please, don't take the journey but fail to claim the prize, this chance to become more of who you really are.

I honour what you've done by choosing to do this work. Many people never deeply engage in this kind of exploration. May you be an inspiration to others, and may you treasure the hard-earned peace and growth you have fought for.

Remember the spiral nature of healing and revisit these pages any time. Thank you for traveling with me. Blessings on your continued journey.

Acknowledgments

Thank you to my publisher, The Experiment, which did such great work with *The Emotionally Absent Mother* and was receptive to my idea of following it up with a workbook. I have been thrilled by the number of foreign translations (eighteen) and their marketing of the first book, and I feel fortunate to be working with them on this new book. I extend my gratitude to the whole team, with special thanks to Matthew Lore at the helm.

Thank you to my editor, Sara Zatopek, who has been with me from the inception of the book through the completion. Thank you, Sara, for responding to my voluminous emails and for being open every time I said, "Oh, wait, I have a new idea!" Thank you for so fiercely advocating for what readers might need and your contributions to the exercises. You put your all into it, and this book is better because of that.

Grace Fern Rychwalski, a new colleague, showed up serendipitously just in time to read my original manuscript before I turned it in. Thank you, Grace, for your valuable feedback and our stimulating exchange of ideas.

My life has always been enriched by those who have shared with me their emotional pain and process, including my clients over many years. You have been part of my path, and what you have taught me is carried forward.

Thank you to the friends who supported me through a process that was bumpy at times—especially Renée Hummel, who was there for me the day I had a meltdown—as well as the larger group that nourishes me and supports my life. And to my bodyworker, Betsy Kabrick, for her amazing support in integrating body, mind, and soul.

All of the therapists I have seen have been an important part of my core journey, but a special shout-out goes to Konstanze Hacker, who not only named my need for an ongoing drip of kindness but also provided so very much more. I wish all of my readers could have this good fortune.

About the Author

JASMIN LEE CORI, MS, practiced as a licensed psychotherapist for many years, specializing in working with adults who experienced childhood abuse and neglect. She has worked in human service agencies and private practice and taught psychology in colleges and professional schools. She is the author of numerous articles and five nonfiction books, including *The Emotionally Absent Mother* and *Healing from Trauma*.

jasmincori.com

Join the Sheldon Press community today, sign up for our newsletter!

- Select a **FREE eBook** or extract to read upon joining

- Keep up with our latest publishing and exciting author news

- Be the first to hear about book prize draws, free extracts, and upcoming author events

Simply scan the QR code below or head to www.sheldonpress.co.uk/newsletter to sign up.